D1483047

Oxycodone

Drugs

ReferencePoint
Press®

San Diego, CA

Other books in the Compact Research Drugs set:

Antidepressants
Club Drugs
Heroin
Marijuana
Painkillers
Prescription Drugs

*For a complete list of titles please visit www.referencepointpress.com.

Oxycodone

Lydia Bjornlund

Drugs

ReferencePoint
Press®

San Diego, CA

© 2012 ReferencePoint Press, Inc.
Printed in the United States

For more information, contact:
ReferencePoint Press, Inc.
PO Box 27779
San Diego, CA 92198
www.ReferencePointPress.com

Picture credits:
Cover: iStockphoto.com
AP Images: 12
Landov: 17
Steve Zmina: 33–35, 47–49,, 62–63, 75–77

LIBRARY OF CONGRESS CATALOGING-IN-PUBLICATION DATA

Bjornlund, Lydia D.
    Oxycodone / by Lydia Bjornlund.
      p. cm. — (Compact research series)
    Includes bibliographical references and index.
    ISBN-13: 978-1-60152-161-3 (hardback)
    ISBN-10: 1-60152-161-8 (hardback)
    1. Oxycodone—Juvenile literature. 2. Oxycodone abuse—Juvenile literature. I. Title.
    RM666.O76B56   2012
    615'.782—dc23
                                                                    2011020202

Contents

Foreword

As modern civilization continues to evolve, its ability to create, store, distribute, and access information expands exponentially. The explosion of information from all media continues to increase at a phenomenal rate. By 2020 some experts predict the worldwide information base will double every 73 days. While access to diverse sources of information and perspectives is paramount to any democratic society, information alone cannot help people gain knowledge and understanding. Information must be organized and presented clearly and succinctly in order to be understood. The challenge in the digital age becomes not the creation of information, but how best to sort, organize, enhance, and present information.

ReferencePoint Press developed the *Compact Research* series with this challenge of the information age in mind. More than any other subject area today, researching current issues can yield vast, diverse, and unqualified information that can be intimidating and overwhelming for even the most advanced and motivated researcher. The *Compact Research* series offers a compact, relevant, intelligent, and conveniently organized collection of information covering a variety of current topics ranging from illegal immigration and deforestation to diseases such as anorexia and meningitis.

The series focuses on three types of information: objective single-author narratives, opinion-based primary source quotations, and facts and statistics. The clearly written objective narratives provide context and reliable background information. Primary source quotes are carefully selected and cited, exposing the reader to differing points of view. And facts and statistics sections aid the reader in evaluating perspectives. Presenting these key types of information creates a richer, more balanced learning experience.

For better understanding and convenience, the series enhances information by organizing it into narrower topics and adding design features that make it easy for a reader to identify desired content. For example, in *Compact Research: Illegal Immigration*, a chapter covering the economic impact of illegal immigration has an objective narrative explaining the various ways the economy is impacted, a balanced section of numerous primary source quotes on the topic, followed by facts and full-color illustrations to encourage evaluation of contrasting perspectives.

The ancient Roman philosopher Lucius Annaeus Seneca wrote, "It is quality rather than quantity that matters." More than just a collection of content, the *Compact Research* series is simply committed to creating, finding, organizing, and presenting the most relevant and appropriate amount of information on a current topic in a user-friendly style that invites, intrigues, and fosters understanding.

Oxycodone at a Glance

Oxycodone Control

Oxycodone is more strictly regulated than other prescription opioids, such as hydrocodone, because of its high risk of addiction and abuse.

Prevalence

The US Drug Enforcement Administration (DEA) reports that some 1.9 million Americans have taken oxycodone for illicit use.

OxyContin on the Street

The most dangerous oxycodone derivative is OxyContin, a brand-name drug that came on the market in 1996. Street names include OC, OX, oxy, oxycotton, ocean, and kicker.

Physical Effects

Like other opioids, oxycodone attaches to specific proteins called opioid receptors, which are found in the brain; opioids diminish the perception of pain.

Addiction

Oxycodone is highly addictive. Many users seek higher and more frequent doses to achieve a feeling of euphoria.

Abuse

Oxycodone abuse has been a problem in the United States since the early 1960s, but abuse escalated following the introduction of OxyContin to the market.

Methods of Abuse

Drug users sometimes crush OxyContin tablets to reverse its intended time-release action, causing more of the drug to enter the bloodstream at once.

Risks Associated with Use

Taken in high quantities, oxycodone can be deadly. In some places fatal overdoses from oxycodone have surpassed automobile accidents as the most common cause of accidental death.

Diversion

OxyContin is among the most commonly diverted prescription drugs. Prescription tampering, pharmacy theft, and faking an illness have all increased as people have sought to obtain the drug.

Weighing Benefits and Risks

OxyContin and other oxycodone products have real benefits for patients in chronic pain. Doctors have to balance the need for addressing pain with the risk of diversion, addiction, and abuse.

Public Perceptions

Many people wrongly assume that oxycodone and other prescription drugs are safer than illegal street drugs.

Prevention Efforts

In April 2011 the White House released a plan to reduce the rate of prescription drug abuse by 15 percent within 5 years. The strategy focuses on 4 main areas: education, monitoring, proper medication disposal, and law enforcement.

Overview

Oxycodone is an opiate, a class of drugs derived from the opium poppy, an agricultural crop valued for food as well as medicine. Oxycodone is a synthetic opiate, meaning that it does not come from the plant itself, but rather is a human-made version that replicates the chemicals found in opium derivatives—in the case of oxycodone, a derivative called thebaine. Opiates such as oxycodone belong to a class of drugs known as narcotics that provide pain relief and induce sleep.

When taken as directed by a doctor, oxycodone provides important medical benefits to patients recovering from surgery or living with chronic pain. Oxycodone is highly addictive, however; patients often begin craving the drug at higher levels than prescribed or for long after the medical need has passed. Oxycodone is also sold on the street to people who use the drug to get a quick high. Some users say taking the drug in large doses provides a high similar to that of heroin. As a result, oxycodone has become the most widely abused painkiller in the United States.

Oxycodone and Pain

Oxycodone is an active ingredient in a variety of prescription medications commonly prescribed to treat moderate to severe pain. Some prescription pain relievers include oxycodone alone; others combine oxycodone with other active ingredients. For example, oxycodone is combined with acetaminophen in Percocet, Tylox, and other name-brand drugs; with aspirin in Percodan, Roxiprin, and others; and with ibuprofen in Combunox.

In addition to its pain-relieving properties, oxycodone can help reduce anxiety and induce sleep. Side effects include feelings of euphoria, constipation, cough suppression, and respiratory depression.

> **While the propensity for abuse had always existed with oxycodone, the development of OxyContin soon ushered in a new era of drug abuse.**

Oxycodone-containing products are in tablet, capsule, and liquid forms. These products are available in a variety of doses, typically prescribed for every four to six hours. Oxycodone is also available in an extended-release form intended for around-the-clock treatment of pain. Originally prescribed to treat the chronic pain associated with terminally ill cancer, the extended-release form of the drug was initially marketed under the brand name OxyContin in 1996.

The Birth of a "Miracle Drug"

Opium is one of the oldest drugs in the world. Artifacts from ancient cultures suggest that opium was used by the Sumerians in 4000 BC and

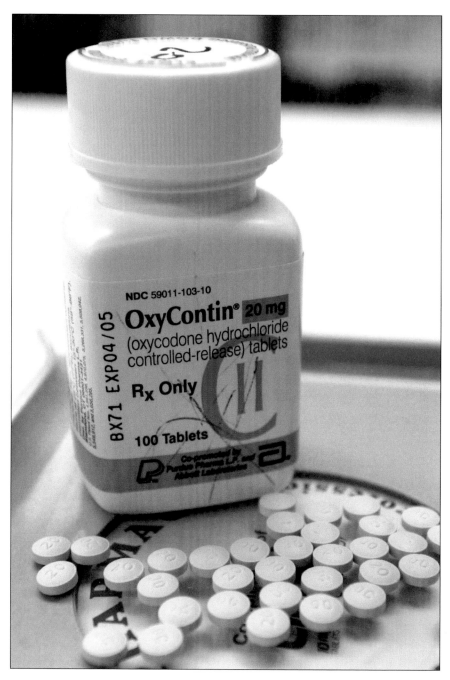

The narcotic drug OxyContin (pictured) can benefit people suffering from chronic pain, but it has also been heavily abused. Soon after its release on the market, users found that they could get an intense high by crushing the tablets or removing the contents of a capsule.

the Egyptians in 2000 BC. Records from Mesopotamian civilizations more than 4,000 years old also refer to the opium poppy. Early healers used an extract from the plant to relieve pain, anxiety, stomach ailments, and problems with vision.

One of the most widely used opiates in modern history is morphine. In the United States morphine was widely used during the Civil War to relieve the pain of soldiers wounded on the battlefield. While morphine and heroin provided much-needed pain relief, they had a number of undesirable side effects, including hallucinations and addiction. As part of the search for an alternative that would be easier to control, scientists at the University of Frankfurt in Germany first synthesized oxycodone in 1916.

> " Often abuse begins when a person becomes addicted to oxycodone that has been prescribed for legitimate purposes. The person may become addicted to the drug, craving increasingly larger doses to achieve the euphoric feeling. "

Oxycodone was introduced in the United States in 1939. Like other opiates, oxycodone was widely prescribed as a pain reliever. The effects of oxycodone typically last four to six hours, requiring patients to continue taking pills during the day. In 1996 Purdue Pharma brought to market a new time-release formula intended to provide long-lasting pain relief. The drug, OxyContin, was hailed as a miracle drug, particularly for cancer patients managing chronic pain. By 2001—in just 5 years—Oxy-Contin had become the best-selling narcotic pain reliever in America, with annual sales topping $1 billion.

How Oxycodone Works

After a drug is taken, it is absorbed into the bloodstream, which carries the drug throughout the body. The drug circulates to organs and tissues. The drug is then carried to the liver, which breaks it down and flushes it away. How long drugs stay in the body—and how long they keep producing their effects—depends on how quickly the drug is broken down and removed. This process is called metabolism. Most drug metabolism takes place in the liver, where enzymes break apart the chemical compound. Metabolism also occurs in the kidneys, lungs, and stomach.

Like other opioids, oxycodone acts by attaching to specific proteins called opioid receptors in the brain and spinal cord. This changes the way a person experiences pain. Opioids also affect parts of the brain that affect the perception of pleasure, providing users with a relaxed, euphoric feeling that some begin to crave. Some experts warn that users gradually build up tolerance to oxycodone and other opioids, so that more of the drug is needed to have the same effect. The combined effect of increased tolerance and continued craving contributes to the risk of addiction and abuse.

From Prescription to Addiction

All drugs derived from opium carry with them the danger of addiction. Opium addiction was so prevalent in China in the 1700s that the Manchu dynasty outlawed the sale of opium under the penalty of death. Says a writer for the American Medical Association (AMA):

> For as long as there have been medicines, the danger of overuse, experimentation and abuse has existed. The rise of patent medicines—based largely on morphine and cocaine—in the middle and late 1800s resulted in one in 200 Americans becoming addicted. These widely used substances were embraced by doctors and patients alike before harm was detected and the first drug control laws were passed.[1]

While the propensity for abuse had always existed with oxycodone, the development of OxyContin soon ushered in a new era of drug abuse. Users found that they could get an intense high by crushing OxyContin tablets or removing the contents of a capsule. Crushing the drug reversed the time-release action, providing a rush of oxycodone into the bloodstream at once. Users say that OxyContin gives the same high as heroin, but is sometimes cheaper with health insurance. The cost of an OxyContin prescription may be covered by health insurance, costing users just pennies per ounce.

From the pharmacy, OxyContin soon hit the street, where it was sold by the pill or by the bottle. People with extra pills from a prescription found they could sell the drug for a big profit. OxyContin quickly rose from a highly touted solution for chronic pain to become the most widely abused drug in the country. Its use in rural areas of Appalachia, where it was widely prescribed to manual laborers suffering from back pain or injuries, earned the drug the moniker "hillbilly heroin." Experts suggest that prescription opioids brought drug abuse into rural areas that had no distribution networks for illegal street drugs like heroin. The epidemic has spread far beyond rural America into urban and suburban homes throughout the United States and Canada.

How Serious a Problem Is Oxycodone Abuse?

For prescription drugs like oxycodone, abuse is defined as the use of the medication in any way that is different from the instructions given by the doctor and/or printed on the label. Prescription drug abuse occurs anytime a drug is used for nonmedical purposes. In 2010 an estimated 5.2 million persons used prescription opioid painkillers for nonmedical purposes.

Often abuse begins when a person becomes addicted to oxycodone that has been prescribed for legitimate purposes. The person may become addicted to the drug, craving increasingly larger doses to achieve the euphoric feeling. An increasing number of oxycodone abusers, however, have never been prescribed oxycodone—they get it from a friend or purchase it on the street specifically for the high that it provides.

Long-lasting forms of oxycodone, such as OxyContin, are the most widely abused form of oxycodone. To get high, users do not simply swallow the pills; they chew OxyContin tablets or mix them into food or drink. An even quicker high can be obtained by crushing and snorting the drug, smoking it off aluminum foil, or injecting it directly into the bloodstream.

> " **Experts warn that early exposure to opioids may interfere with brain development, which continues until the mid-twenties or so. Abusing oxycodone as a teen may therefore have lifelong consequences.** "

Different people react to oxycodone differently. Some people take high doses of the drug for weeks without becoming addicted, while others seem to crave more of the drug almost immediately. This difference in part stems from differences in people's metabolism. In older people, for instance, the liver and other organs function less effectively, so they do not metabolize drugs the same way as younger adults. People with a serious illness also may have reduced liver function, which makes them more susceptible to adverse side effects.

> **Many oxycodone addicts who want to quit find it impossible to do so without help. Withdrawal from longtime use of the drug can create highly unpleasant side effects, including muscle and bone pain, diarrhea, vomiting, and cold flashes with goose bumps.**

Studies suggest that there may be a genetic component to addiction—people whose parents are dependent on drugs may be at greater risk of drug abuse and dependency themselves. Other factors that may influence the potential of drug abuse include the social environment, family and peer influences, and the price and availability of drugs. A recent study published in the *Archives of Pediatrics & Adolescent Medicine* found that teens who are in poor health, suffer from depression, or use other drugs were at greater risk of prescription drug abuse. The study further found that living in a household with two parents decreased the odds of such use by 32 percent. Some studies have found a link between oxycodone abuse and childhood abuse or neglect. In one study, nearly two-thirds of people in treatment programs for OxyContin abuse reported that they were physically or sexually abused as children.

What Are the Health Dangers of Oxycodone?

Oxycodone abuse can be deadly. Taken repeatedly or in high doses, oxycodone can cause severe anxiety, paranoia, hallucinations, insomnia, irregular or slow heart rate, and seizures. Overdose of oxycodone can result in coma or severe respiratory depression or arrest, a fatal event in which a person stops breathing.

The risks are multiplied when oxycodone is taken with alcohol or other drugs. Oxycodone increases the effect of drugs that slow brain function, such as alcohol, antihistamines, barbiturates, muscle relaxants, benzodiazepines, and sleeping pills. Taking oxycodone in combination with any of these drugs puts people at risk of a life-threatening problem.

Young people also are at greater risk of the adverse effects of oxycodone. Experts warn that early exposure to opioids may interfere with brain development, which continues until the mid-twenties or so. Abusing oxycodone as a teen may therefore have lifelong consequences.

Treatment and Recovery

Many oxycodone addicts who want to quit find it impossible to do so without help. Withdrawal from longtime use of the drug can create

A young woman gazes out of the window of a North Carolina institution where she is being treated for OxyContin and alcohol abuse. Severe anxiety, paranoia, hallucinations, irregular or slow heart rate, and seizures can result from abuse of the drug. The effects are compounded by alcohol abuse.

highly unpleasant side effects, including muscle and bone pain, diarrhea, vomiting, and cold flashes with goose bumps. Users often exhibit calm, relaxed behavior while on the drug, but then experience wild mood swings, intense sensitivity to light and sound, delusions and/or hallucinations, and heightened pain (sometimes imagined). Oxycodone and withdrawal from the drug can also disrupt sleep patterns, resulting in insomnia and/or sudden sleepiness.

Treatment for oxycodone abuse often typically involves gradually weaning the user off the drug in a process known as detoxification. Sometimes the detoxification process involves replacing the oxycodone use with another drug that provides a similar effect, thereby reducing the adverse effects of quitting. Currently used medications include methadone and buprenorphine, which are synthetic opioids that have been used to treat heroin addiction.

> **Making the drug available to patients in real pain while keeping it out of the hands of addicts and illegal drug dealers has proved to be a difficult balancing act.**

Treatment experts emphasize that treating the physical addiction alone may have little impact. Behavioral strategies are often a key part of a successful treatment program. These strategies teach patients how to handle cravings, the importance of avoiding drugs and situations that could lead to drug use, and preventing and handling relapses. Therapy that helps people cope with stress can also aid recovery. Support groups in which opioid addicts can share their stories of addiction and the path to recovery are sometimes essential tools as well.

Should the Government Do More to Control Oxycodone?

The main law controlling oxycodone (and other drugs) is the Controlled Substances Act of 1970. The act created five categories—or schedules—of drugs based on criteria such as a drug's accepted medical uses and its potential for abuse and addiction. Because of the high risk of addiction and abuse, oxycodone is classified as a Schedule II drug. Schedule II drugs have the highest potential for abuse of any approved drugs. In comparison, hydrocodone (the opioid in Vicodin) and several lesser-known opioid painkillers are Schedule III drugs, which are not as strictly regulated.

As a Schedule II drug, oxycodone is highly regulated. A prescription for oxycodone cannot be called into a pharmacy or filled by mail order. The patient must take a valid written prescription into a pharmacy to be filled. In addition, no refills can be given for oxycodone prescriptions; a doctor must write a new prescription each time. These measures are intended to help monitor the drug and ensure it is used as prescribed, thereby reducing the availability of the drug for abuse.

The Balancing Act

Unlike illegal street drugs such as heroin, oxycodone is a legal substance when prescribed and taken appropriately. Making the drug available to patients in real pain while keeping it out of the hands of addicts and illegal drug dealers has proved to be a difficult balancing act. The difficulty is compounded by unscrupulous doctors enticed by the great sums of money that illegally prescribing oxycodone can bring and online pharmacies that provide painkillers without a prescription. On the other hand, some doctors accused of overprescribing oxycodone may believe that they are providing proper treatment for a patient who is truly in pain.

Pain management specialists and patients say that the impact of stringent law enforcement activities intended to address drug abuse may interfere with patients' ability to access medicine that they need to cope with very real pain. According to the American Academy of Pain Medicine, an estimated 70 million Americans have experienced chronic pain at some point in their life, and many of these need some form of pain medication to carry out everyday tasks of living. Moreover, as the population ages, pain medication may be in greater demand.

The increasing use of prescription narcotics by Americans may be a contributing factor to the abuse of these drugs. Doctors find themselves balancing the need to address the real pain of patients against the reality that some people may seek the drug for recreational purposes—or for sale to others. "Most of the patients I see, probably 90 percent, have legitimate pain. The challenge is figuring out who's who,"[2] says Dr. Moshe Lewis, a pain management specialist with the California Pacific Medical Center in San Francisco.

Robert L. DuPont, president of the Institute for Behavior and Health, a nonprofit drug abuse policy organization, says doctors are more apt to give pain relievers than in the past. "Before the last decade, doctors were very reluctant to prescribe these medications to outpatients. But because of concern about the undertreatment of pain, their prescription has become ubiquitous."[3] Antidrug advocates say that liberal prescribing policies have flooded the market with illegal narcotics. "We hate to see somebody in pain run out of medicine, so sometimes we may be a little too generous,"[4] admits Kyle Kampman, the medical director of the Charles O'Brien Center for Addiction Treatment at the University of Pennsylvania.

> **Many doctors say they are reluctant to prescribe prescription pain relievers—especially oxycodone—because of the risk of addiction.**

Still, many doctors say they are reluctant to prescribe prescription pain relievers—especially oxycodone—because of the risk of addiction. "I have colleagues who are board certified in pain who will not write significant pain medication for treatment," says Lewis. "Many of them are feeling overwhelmed and scared."[5]

How Can Oxycodone Abuse Be Prevented?

Education is one of the most important aspects of any prevention program, and this may be particularly true of a drug that is initially prescribed for a valid reason. Most prescription drugs come with a package insert that provides detailed product information, including potential risks and side effects. The information is intended to protect patients from unintentional misuse. The FDA also requires warning labels—called "black box labels"—to be included for drugs with potentially serious side effects. The OxyContin label carries a warning about the drug's potential for addiction or abuse.

Preventing drug abuse requires combating its root causes and addressing the recreational use of the drug. Because most users first try prescription painkillers at a young age, many prevention efforts target teens. School-based antidrug programs reach into schools of all sizes and types. Drug Abuse Resistance Education—or D.A.R.E.—is perhaps the largest and best-known school-based antidrug program. More than 100,000 police officers participate in D.A.R.E. programs, reaching into the classrooms of about 5,000 children a year. Many thousands of packets of educational materials and other aids are distributed to teachers and parents. Objectives include teaching children how to identify drugs and explaining their effects and dangers. One key message is to resist peer pressure by refusing offers of drugs.

In addition, a number of public and private organizations use a variety of media—television ads, print material, and the Internet—to inform young people of the harmful consequences of prescription drugs. The Partnership for a Drug-Free America, for example, operates a website that includes multimedia activities designed to influence the attitudes and behaviors of young people.

Prevention efforts must also address the widespread availability of oxycodone products. Many parents and teens alike are unaware of the very real dangers of prescription painkillers. Educating parents and other adults who are prescribed prescription painkillers about their dangers and providing tips for safe disposal may be important strategies for keeping the drugs out of the hands of young people.

Prognosis for the Future

Government organizations, schools, and the medical profession are coming together to address the abuse of oxycodone, using many of the same strategies that have been instrumental in decreasing the use of street drugs. Success will depend on addressing both the supply of and demand for the drug. An important first step is educating patients, teens, and other at-risk populations of the very real dangers of prescription drug abuse.

How Serious a Problem Is Oxycodone Abuse?

66 **Prescription drug abuse is the fastest growing drug problem in the United States, with prescription drugs ranking behind marijuana as the second-most abused category of drugs.** 99

> —Office of National Drug Control Policy, the White House office responsible for setting the nation's drug control policy.

66 **When a patient walks out of the doctor's office, a single, daily dose can be sold on the street for $100. So if a person comes out . . . with a prescription for 30 pills, that's $3,000. . . . You think about how many people are attracted to that, to those economics, never mind the biology of it. And you get some idea of the potential for this as a major public health threat.** 99

> —Robert L. DuPont, former director of NIDA and a leading authority on drug prevention and treatment.

The nonmedical use of oxycodone—or oxycodone abuse—means using the drug in any way that is different than prescribed. Some patients who have been prescribed the drug to meet a legitimate need abuse the drug by taking it in greater quantities or at greater frequency than prescribed. Other abusers take oxycodone that has been prescribed to someone else. Regardless of whether the user takes oxycodone at higher levels than prescribed to address chronic pain or accepts a few pills from a friend to get a quick high, using a drug without a prescription is against the law. With oxycodone, it can also be deadly.

The Rise of an Epidemic

The first widespread abuse of OxyContin appeared in the hills of Appalachia, where it was widely prescribed to treat back pain and other chronic ailments. OxyContin got its moniker "hillbilly heroin" from early use in these rural areas of Appalachia, but the oxycodone epidemic soon took hold among middle- and upper-class Americans, who could afford the high prices often charged on the street. Today the drug is popular among professionals in cities and suburbs across America. Middle- and upper-class Americans may be lured to OxyContin by its legal status, which makes taking it—even in large quantities—seem less dangerous and immoral than using illegal street drugs.

Still, many poor, rural communities continue to struggle with higher-than-average rates of OxyContin abuse. Experts suggest that this may be due to the fact that prescription drugs may be more accessible than street drugs in rural communities, which have pharmacies but no criminal networks for illegal drugs. Abuse rates are also alarmingly high in a number of East Coast cities—including New York City and Boston. The *Wall Street Journal* reported that the number of oxycodone prescriptions in New York City doubled in just three years, between 2007 and 2010. In 2010 more than 1 million prescriptions for oxycodone were filled in the 5 boroughs, amounting to roughly 1 prescription for every 8 people. Experts say that prescriptions are fueling the illicit use of the drug and represent a sign that the drug is being diverted for abuse.

Populations at Risk

With OxyContin and other oxycodone products, abuse often begins when people have been prescribed a drug and continue to crave it after their problem has been treated. This is what happened when Santino Quaranta, the youngest player ever drafted to play professional soccer, was prescribed painkillers after an injury. Quaranta got hooked on prescription painkillers because they made him feel good—an addiction that nearly cost him his professional soccer career. "It wasn't an instant addiction," says Quaranta. "It was on and off. I don't know when I crossed the line, but it really got bad. I was a mess."[6]

Sometimes abuse begins like with any other illegal drug, with people seeking a recreational high. Researchers suggest that the fact that prescription drugs are approved for use by the government and doctors may make users assume that they are safer than illegal street drugs, but the statistics on drug interactions and overdoses suggests otherwise.

Young people appear to be particularly at risk of oxycodone abuse. Opioid pain relievers like oxycodone have become the drug of choice on many college and high school campuses, second only to marijuana. Oxycodone products are often sought out by teens engaged in "pharming," a dangerous trend in which users take handfuls of pills, often chased by beer or other alcohol.

Doctor Shopping

To get a higher dosage of drugs than any one doctor would typically prescribe, patients—or people posing as patients—sometimes see several physicians. This practice is referred to as "doctor shopping." Perhaps the most highly publicized incident of doctor shopping involved the 2003 arrest of Rush Limbaugh, a conservative talk show host. Limbaugh allegedly obtained over 2,000 prescription narcotics over a six-month period.

> **The first widespread abuse of OxyContin appeared in the hills of Appalachia, where it was widely prescribed to treat back pain and other chronic ailments.**

To counter the risk of abuse, some doctors and pain management clinics require patients to sign an oath that they will not obtain prescriptions elsewhere, but the requirements are hard to enforce. "When you're addicted to drugs, you're going to do whatever you have to do to get that drug," says a police officer in Austin, Texas. "And if it means you're going to go to the next doctor and sign the same piece of paper, then you're going to do that."[7]

Not all doctor shoppers are seeking the drugs for their own use. Drug traffickers have created elaborate ruses to trick doctors and pharmacies into writing prescriptions for drugs that they then sell on the street. One such dealer paid homeless people in California to pose as patients and then resold the narcotics they obtained at great profit. Others may fool doctors into prescribing painkillers for weeks or months by claiming they have medical conditions or ailments that are hard to diagnose, such as toothaches or kidney pain.

Occasionally, people with a legitimate medical need to oxycodone are lured by the promise of great profits to use their prescription for financial gain. In Tucson, Arizona, for example, one man took advantage of a severe medical condition to obtain legitimate prescriptions for OxyContin and other oxycodone products from several different physicians and then filled the prescriptions at various pharmacies. The tablets, approximately 8,000 to 9,000 over the course of a year, were sent via FedEx to another individual in Maryland, who then sold them on the street at a substantial profit.

> To get a higher dosage of drugs than any one doctor would typically prescribe, patients—or people posing as patients—sometimes see several physicians.

Forgery and Theft

People addicted to oxycodone often go to great lengths to get the drug. "Once patients are addicted," explains author Melody Petersen, "they change in ways that no one could have expected. Even people with families and good jobs have turned to crime to get the pills their bodies crave."[8]

Patients may alter a legitimate prescription to increase the amount of oxycodone pills on the prescription, the dosage, or the number of refills—a felony offense that in some states is as easy as writing over what is on the prescription or circling a different number of refills on the prescription. Others forge the prescription pads themselves, using a counterfeiter's skills to re-create the look of a legal prescription. In 2011, 12 people in Prince William County, Virginia, for instance, were arrested for forging prescriptions. According to the affidavit, the members of the drug ring used computer templates to copy prescriptions and information from real doctors. They then forged the prescriptions for oxycodone with the real names of people whose driver's licenses they had stolen and sold the pills in smaller quantities out of their own homes.

Some addicts resort to violence. Recent years have witnessed a rapid increase in the number of pharmacy robberies. More than 1,800 robberies of US pharmacies occurred in just 3 years, from 2008 to 2010. In 2001, Edmonton, Alberta, Canada, experienced 11 pharmacy robberies in just 3 months, and oxycodone was the main target. In Biddeford, Maine, the same pharmacy was struck 3 times in just 1 year by a robber demanding OxyContin. In Tulsa, Oklahoma, where pharmacy robberies far outpace bank robberies, police say the perpetrators have shifted from addicts in search of a fix to gangs looking for opioids to sell on the street. The author of a 2011 *New York Times* article writes:

> The robbers are brazen and desperate. In Rockland, Me., one wielded a machete as he leapt over a pharmacy counter to snatch the painkiller oxycodone, gulping some before he fled. In Satellite Beach, Fla., a robber threatened a pharmacist with a cordless drill last week, and in North Highlands, Calif., a holdup last summer led to a shootout that left a pharmacy worker dead.[9]

Drug Rings and Gangs

The illegal trade of oxycodone has given rise to interstate distribution rings and local gangs that mirror the supply chains of other illicit drugs. According to a 2010 report of the National Drug Intelligence Center (NDIC), "More law enforcement agencies are reporting that pharmaceutical diversion and abuse pose the greatest drug threat to their areas, in part because of increases in associated crime and gang involvement, which put additional strain on agency budgets and assets."[10] Law enforcement agencies suggest that oxycodone abuse is responsible for at least half of this criminal activity.

Some of the drug rings are led by doctors or pharmacists, who work in clinics that law enforcement officials call "pill mills." Pill mill clinics vary greatly, but an increasing number are disguised as independent pain management centers. Pill mills differ from legitimate medical facilities because they do not screen patients to assess whether the request for painkillers is to meet real pain. Most pill mills accept only cash; some patients leave with the drugs in hand without ever seeing a doctor. The doctors at such facilities do not work with patients to consider alternative pain relief strategies—their goal is not to treat patients but rather to sell painkillers. Some pill mills attract patients from thousands of miles away, where painkillers are more difficult to obtain. In some communities neighbors complain of drug addicts lining up at the doors of pain management clinics waiting for the office to open.

The DEA has cracked down on pill mills, but many run for years without being investigated. To avoid detection, the operations often open and close quickly and move doctors from one part of the country to another. "These guys are very, very good at staying under the radar," says Andrea Trescot, a leading pain specialist. "It is a huge societal problem. What they're causing are patients to get addicted and potentially die."[11]

> Drug traffickers have created elaborate ruses to trick doctors and pharmacies into writing prescriptions for drugs that they then sell on the street.

Not all of the drug rings are led by doctors, however. In Boston the defendants indicted for the sale of OxyContin included the aide to the mayor. In New York City an OxyContin drug ring was run out of an ice cream truck on Staten Island. Before the bust, the dealers had sold 42,755 pills at upwards of $20 each, earning them more than $1 million a year. The ringleaders forged prescriptions for the pills and then had addicts fill them at nearby pharmacies in exchange for a few of the pills. Records show that the dealers paid an average of just $1.66 per pill. One of the things that made the bust alarming is that it took place right under the noses of citizens in an upscale neighborhood. "This ring was operating in the safest police precinct in New York City," said the district attorney of the Staten Island district. "We are equating this to the beginning of an epidemic similar to when crack cocaine was first introduced."[12]

Effect on Society

In some areas the overuse and abuse of OxyContin and other oxycodone products have been blamed for sudden spikes in crime, putting a strain on all aspects of the criminal justice system, including local police, courts, and prisons. Opiates can cause paranoia and an altered sense of reality, which may lead some people to engage in violent behavior. Some people also become agitated when coming down from an opiate high and may be frustrated or frightened by the prospect of not having more of the drug. Experts blame OxyContin abuse and addiction for a growing number of domestic violence and spousal abuse episodes. Meanwhile, victims of domestic violence might start buying OxyContin to deal with the abuse, expanding the vicious circle of dependence, abuse, addiction, and violence.

> In some areas the overuse and abuse of OxyContin and other oxycodone products have been blamed for sudden spikes in crime, putting a strain on all aspects of the criminal justice system, including local police, courts, and prisons.

In Greenup County, Kentucky, a small rural community with a population of just 1,200, the sheriff says that it is impossible to keep up with the epidemic. The county jail holds twice the number of inmates as a decade ago, and Sheriff Jeff Cooper says that more than 90 percent of the people incarcerated have committed crimes that are related to oxycodone in one way or another: "Whether its burglary to get pills, theft to get pills, spousal abuse because they're on pills, DUI because of pills . . . just about all of [the arrests] . . . one way or another, has to do with pills. . . . Literally every family in this county has been affected one way or another."[13]

Problems stemming from oxycodone addiction are widespread and extend far beyond the stereotypical drug user. Many abusers have lost jobs, family, and friends as a result of their addiction. Oxycodone addiction alone costs the country billions of dollars a year, mostly in lost productivity due to increased health problems, sick leave, and hospitalization.

How Serious a Problem Is Oxycodone Abuse?

66 Opioid medicines are basically a societal good, with a potential for diversion and harm to the public health. 99

—William Colby, "Balance, Uniformity, and Fairness: Effective Strategies for Law Enforcement for Investigating and Prosecuting the Diversion of Prescription Pain Medications While Protecting Appropriate Medical Practice," Center for Practical Bioethics, September 2009. www.practicalbioethics.org.

Colby is a lawyer at the Center for Practical Bioethics.

66 [OxyContin] is a horrible drug and it is ruining our lives! I am only 18 years old and I have been addicted for almost 2 years. . . . I was hooked the first time I tried it! 99

—Samantha, "Oxycontin Addiction, Abuse and Treatment," Addiction Search, September 22, 2010. www.addictionsearch.com.

At just 18 years of age, Samantha is already a victim of OxyContin addiction.

* Editor's Note: While the definition of a primary source can be narrowly or broadly defined, for the purposes of Compact Research, a primary source consists of: 1) results of original research presented by an organization or researcher; 2) eyewitness accounts of events, personal experience, or work experience; 3) first-person editorials offering pundits' opinions; 4) government officials presenting political plans and/or policies; 5) representatives of organizations presenting testimony or policy.

Primary Source Quotes

66 Oxycontin addiction has many faces. It could be resid- ing next door in the guise of your neighbor. It could be present in the mailroom clerk at your office. Oxycon- tin addiction could be hiding behind the angst of your teenager or even in your own reflection in a mirror. 99

—Drug Alcohol Rehab, "Oxycontin Addiction," 2011. www.drugalcohol-rehab.com.

The Drug Alcohol Rehab website is run by a group of substance abuse advocates who seek to provide accurate information about drug abuse and addiction.

66 Today, far too many of our loved ones are addicted [to OxyContin]. They commit crimes to feed this power- ful addiction and are funneled through our courts and jails at great expense, destined only to return. 99

—Therese Murray and Steven A. Tolman, "Prisons Alone Won't Win War on Drugs," BostonHerald.com, March 16, 2011. www.bostonherald.com.

Murray is president of the Massachusetts Senate; Tolman is a Massachusetts state senator from Brighton.

66 Most pill addicts will drive to China to find a doc- tor that will prescribe . . . OxyContin [and other opi- oids]. Nothing will stop the addict determined to get pills—nothing. 99

—Todd A. Zalkins, *Dying for Triplicate: A True Story of Addiction, Survival, and Recovery*. Scotts Valley, CA: CreateSpace, 2010.

Zalkins wrote a book about his experience with prescription drugs and his strug- gle to beat an addiction to OxyContin.

66 The tremendous potential profits from selling prescrip- tion opioids ensure a long-standing problem, especially since otherwise law-abiding citizens are contributing to the illicit drug market to make ends meet. 99

—Marvin Seppala, *Prescription Painkillers: History, Pharmacology, and Treatment*. Center City, MN: Hazelden, 2010.

Seppala is chief medical officer at Hazelden, a network of substance abuse treat- ment facilities, and serves as adjunct assistant professor at the Hazelden Gradu- ate School of Addiction Studies.

> **❝I'm middle aged with severe arthritis and I take oxy AS PRESCRIBED, it allows me to function and be mobile.❞**

—Don, "Oxycontin Addiction, Abuse and Treatment," Addiction Search, September 22, 2010. www.addictionsearch.com.

Don used the message board at Addiction Search to defend the ability of oxycodone users to obtain the drug.

> **❝Studies have shown that, for many, prescription drugs are the very first drugs they abuse—and all too often they aren't the last.❞**

—Michele M. Leonhart, quoted in "DEA Holding Second Nationwide Prescription Drug Take-Back Day in April," DEA news release, March 8, 2011. www.justice.gov.

Leonhart is the administrator of the DEA.

Facts and Illustrations

How Serious a Problem Is Oxycodone Abuse?

- Americans make up just **4.6 percent** of the world's population but consume **80 percent** of the supply of narcotic painkillers. More than **3 percent** of Americans receive long-term therapy with opioid pain relievers for chronic noncancer pain.

- OxyContin is America's top-selling opioid. In 2009 it accounted for **$2.9 billion** in sales for Purdue Pharma.

- More people abuse prescription painkillers than heroin, cocaine, and ecstasy combined. Roughly **75 percent** of all prescription drug abuse involves painkillers.

- According to the National Survey on Drug Use and Health estimates, in 2009 roughly **584,000 Americans** used OxyContin without a prescription for the first time.

- Those who commit **oxycodone abuse** at least once or use other painkillers tend to cluster around the age group of about 16 to 49. The average age at first use in 2009 was 22.3 years, according to the National Survey on Drug Use and Health.

- According to the 2009 Monitoring the Future study, **4.9 percent** of high school seniors have taken OxyContin without a prescription.

Abuse of Opioid Pain Relievers Is Second Only to Marijuana

As pharmaceutical companies find new drugs to combat a wide range of illnesses, the number of people who abuse these drugs has grown exponentially. Prescription pain relievers are particularly problematic: Many users become addicted to these drugs and continue using them long past when they are needed. Pain relievers are also sought out by recreational drug users seeking a high. Today, more Americans illegally use prescription painkillers than any other drug except marijuana.

Number Who Illegally Used Drugs in 2009

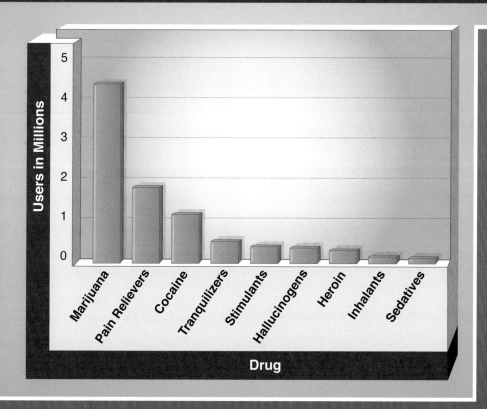

Source: Substance Abuse and Mental Health Services Administration, "Results from the 2009 National Survey on Drug Use and Health: Summary of National Findings," September 2010. http://oas.samhsa.gov.

33

OxyContin Abuse Among Twelfth Graders

Experts are concerned that a growing number of teens are abusing OxyContin. More than 1 in 20 twelfth graders have used OxyContin without a prescription in the last year. While a lower percentage of teens appear to use the drug today than in 2005, the use of the drug has risen 1.1 percent since 2002, while the use of most other illegal substances has declined.

Percentage of twelfth graders who have used OxyContin in the past year

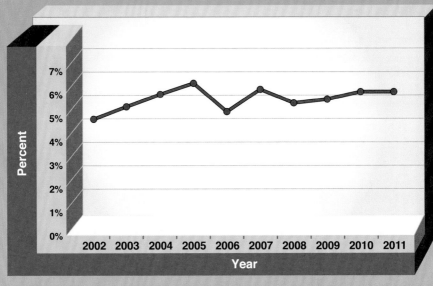

Source: Lloyd D. Johnston et al., *Monitoring the Future: National Results on Adolescent Drug Use, 2010*, National Institute on Drug Abuse, February 2011.

- A study published in November 2010 found that rural teens are **26 percent** more likely to use prescription drugs for nonmedical purposes than are urban teens; rural and urban teens have the same rate of abuse of illegal drugs such as marijuana, heroin, cocaine, and hallucinogens.

The Cost of Oxycodone Abuse

A 2011 study estimates the cost of nonmedical use of prescription opioids to be $53.4 billion in 2006, of which OxyContin and oxycodone amounted to $13.3 billion. Most of these costs are attributable to lost productivity, such as when people are out sick, hospitalized, or in rehab programs for drug abuse.

Cost of Prescription Opioid Abuse

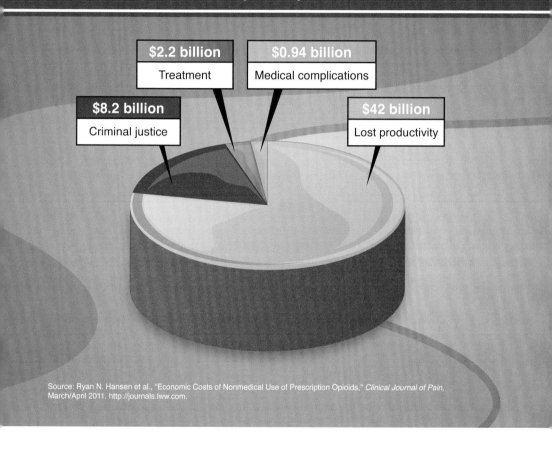

$2.2 billion
Treatment

$0.94 billion
Medical complications

$8.2 billion
Criminal justice

$42 billion
Lost productivity

Source: Ryan N. Hansen et al., "Economic Costs of Nonmedical Use of Prescription Opioids," *Clinical Journal of Pain*, March/April 2011. http://journals.lww.com.

- In a 2010 study conducted by Washington University School of Medicine in St. Louis, Missouri, over **50 percent** of retired professional football players said they used prescription painkillers while playing.

What Are the Health Dangers of Oxycodone Abuse?

❝OxyContin is essentially heroin, just made in a lab, and because it's pharmaceutically pure, it's even more addictive.❞

—Natalie Morales, journalist and narrator of the "Hillbilly Heroin" episode of A&E's *Intervention*.

❝The vast majority of unintentional drug overdose deaths are not the result of toddlers getting into medicines or the elderly mixing up their pills. All available evidence suggests that these deaths are related to the increasing use of prescription drugs, especially opioid painkillers.❞

—Leonard J. Paulozzi, medical epidemiologist at the Centers for Disease Control and Prevention (CDC).

Oxycodone is a highly effective drug when used according to a prescription, but it poses significant risks when taken by people who are not under a doctor's care. Oxycodone is especially dangerous when taken to get high, because it is usually taken in larger quantities than would be prescribed. Crushing OxyContin to negate its long-lasting action adds a new level of risk. The label required for OxyContin warns of the dangers of abuse: "OxyContin must be swallowed whole and must not be cut, broken, chewed, crushed or dissolved. Taking cut, broken, chewed, crushed or dissolved OxyContin tablets leads to rapid release and absorption of a potentially fatal dose of oxycodone."[14]

Side Effects

More than one-quarter of patients taking oxycodone complain of constipation; 10 to 25 percent also experience drowsiness, nausea, and/or dizziness. Doctors caution that these side effects may impact a person's ability to drive or operate heavy machinery. The use of alcohol, sedatives, and many other drugs multiplies these risks. Asthma and sleep apnea also put people at greater risk of dangerous side effects.

The risks increase with increased dosage. The US National Library of Medicine warns: "Oxycodone 60-mg tablets and oxycodone 160-mg tablets (not available in the United States) should only be used to treat people who are tolerant (used to the effects of a medication) to narcotic pain medication. These tablet strengths may cause serious breathing problems or death in people who are not tolerant to narcotics."[15]

> " Researchers at the CDC found that women who use opioid painkillers just before they got pregnant or in the first trimester of pregnancy were more likely to have a baby born with [birth defects]. "

Elderly patients, who do not metabolize drugs as well as younger people, and women who are pregnant or plan to become pregnant need to be cautious about the use of these drugs. Experts also worry about the impact of the drug on young people, because the human brain is not fully developed until people are in their mid-twenties.

Health Risks

Long-term use of oxycodone increases the risk of health effects. The drug causes high blood pressure in some people, which can lead to serious heart problems, heart attack, or stroke.

Like other drugs, oxycodone can cause liver problems. The liver is particularly vulnerable to drug abuse because it is where much of the drug metabolism takes place and where enzymes break apart the chemical compound. Oxycodone also sometimes causes bleeding in the stomach or intestines. While the risk is higher among people who smoke cigarettes or drink alcohol, problems sometimes occur suddenly and without warning. Doctors warn that the result can be fatal.

> **Smoking crushed OxyContin off aluminum foil or injecting it directly into the bloodstream increases the risk of serious adverse effects over the short and the long term.**

Frequent use of oxycodone can also cause behavioral problems. Some users experience hallucinations and delusions. Abusers may be calm when on the drug but become extremely agitated or volatile when coming down from the high. Some users are extremely sensitive to light and/or sound and experience increasingly extreme mood swings.

Long-term use of oxycodone also has been associated with increased risk of depression and other mental illness. Some experts believe that oxycodone and other opioids may reduce inhibitions and increase anxiety or paranoia, which in turn contribute to a user's inclination for violence or other criminal behavior.

Use During Pregnancy

Oxycodone may also present problems for pregnant women and unborn fetuses. Some studies suggest that the drug may cause infertility or increase the risk of miscarriage.

Babies born to mothers who took oxycodone while pregnant may exhibit respiratory problems and are at greater risk of congenital heart defects, which is the primary birth defect leading to infant death in the United States. In a study published in 2011, researchers at the CDC further found that women who use opioid painkillers just before they got pregnant or in the first trimester of pregnancy were more likely to have a baby born with spina bifida (a type of neural tube defect), hydrocephaly (a buildup of fluid in the brain), glaucoma (an eye disease), or gastroschisis (a defect of the abdominal wall). In addition, studies have shown adverse effects among breast-feeding infants of mothers who are taking oxycodone.

Infants of mothers who take oxycodone during pregnancy often experience painful withdrawal symptoms during the first few weeks of life. Doctors warn that other health problems may emerge among these infants as they grow up. Some experts believe that babies born to OxyContin abusers may be at greater risk than the general population to drug addiction or mental illness as adults.

Overdose

Overdose is a very real danger of abusing oxycodone. The risk of fatal overdose increases with increasing doses, a sudden increase in the dose taken, and increasing frequency of use. Taking oxycodone in combination with alcohol, sedatives, or other depressants also increases the risk of a fatal adverse reaction.

Oxycodone does not discriminate between new recreational users and longtime addicts. Brett Tozzo, a 22-year-old personal trainer in Sarasota, Florida, died within just four months of trying OxyContin "because he was full of aches and pains,"[16] says a friend. In addition to OxyContin, an autopsy after his death found alcohol and heroin in his system; his family says it was his foray into OxyContin that led him to heroin use.

Tozzo is just one of many victims. In the United States drug-related poisonings are the second leading cause of accidental deaths, second only to automobile accidents; they are the leading cause in 17 states and the District of Columbia.

> **When they cannot find a doctor who will prescribe their desired drug, otherwise honest people may turn to dealers who sell oxycodone on the street.**

In OxyContin-infested communities the death rate from drug overdose is staggering. In Scioto County, Ohio, for instance, OxyContin abuse results in almost one death every week, and drug overdoses surpass car accidents as the leading cause of accidental death. Reporters say that very few families have escaped the pain caused by the epidemic. "The devil is running Scioto County," says Governor John Kasich. "There is so much pain, death, addiction. We have a war going within our own borders, and it's coming out of pharmacies, doctor's offices, pill mills making a profit from selling poison to our citizens."[17]

Smoking and Injecting Oxycodone

Oxycodone abusers usually begin by taking the drug orally, but some move on to other, more dangerous drug delivery methods. Smoking crushed OxyContin off aluminum foil or injecting it directly into the bloodstream increases the risk of serious adverse effects over the short and the long term.

> " In OxyContin-infested communities the death rate from drug overdose is staggering. "

As with any drug that is injected, there is also the danger associated with needles. Intravenous use of any drug can result in infectious diseases such as HIV/AIDS and hepatitis C, which if left untreated leads to liver disease. Massachusetts leaders have blamed the recent spike in the hepatitis C virus on increasing OxyContin abuse. "My boyfriend almost lost his life due to a staph infection from an old needle," writes a guest blogger who spent a year in rehab to get over her OxyContin addiction. "He had to have heart and lung surgery and dialysis."[18]

Addiction and Abuse: When the User Cannot Quit

Much of the risk of oxycodone is related to its highly addictive qualities. While many experts say the drug is not addictive when used as prescribed, many patients build up a tolerance to the drug and find that higher doses are needed to manage the pain for which the drug was prescribed. Patients with tendencies for substance abuse may begin to crave the feeling of euphoria brought on by the drug. Research suggests that some people are at far greater risk of becoming dependent on drugs than others. For this reason, doctors emphasize that it is important to avoid giving oxycodone to anyone with a history of substance abuse.

With high doses of oxycodone, unpleasant withdrawal symptoms may occur if the user stops taking the drug. "Every muscle in your body craves it," says Jeff Trapp, who became addicted to OxyContin after a spinal injury. "You can't sleep, can't eat. It's like the flu, but 10 times worse."[19]

Some addicts become so dependent on drugs that they may fake an injury or illness to obtain them. When they cannot find a doctor who will prescribe their desired drug, otherwise honest people may turn to dealers who sell oxycodone on the street. Santino Quaranta tells of his efforts to fuel his addiction: "Even when the doctors gave me pills, it was just 20 or 30. I would go through those in a couple hours. I would eat 10 at a time. There weren't enough pills in the world for me. You could have put me in Iraq and I would have found a way to get pills. I should have been dead a long time ago."[20] Following a long struggle with addiction that almost cost him his professional soccer career, Quaranta today chooses to play through excruciating pain rather than take prescription painkillers.

> **Experts worry that Percocet, OxyContin, or other oxycodone products may serve as gateway drugs to abuse of other dangerous and illegal drugs, most notably heroin.**

Pharming: Oxycodone as a Party Drug

Oxycodone is among the drugs of choice for young people as well. Like other narcotic drugs, oxycodone has become part of a trend called pharming, in which teens search their parents' medicine cabinets for drugs to share with their friends. Pharming parties, at which teens swallow handfuls of prescription drugs, often chased by beer or other alcohol, are a dangerous trend. Steve Hayes, the director of a treatment center in the Midwest, explains:

> Some of our patients . . . tell us about parties that kids as young as 11 attend. Instead of bringing a present, each child is to bring some prescription drugs that they got from their parents' medicine cabinet. When they arrive at the party, they go into a room and pour the drugs into a punch bowl. Then the kids will take turns reaching into the bowl and taking a handful of pills. Sometimes the kids combine this with alcohol—an often lethal combination.[21]

Pharming does not always occur at parties. At one school in Texas, nine middle school students were hospitalized when a teacher reported slurred speech and sleepiness among several students who had taken prescription drugs freely offered by another student. "Somebody showed up with some [prescription drugs], a lot, and just started handing them out like candy," said the chief of police. "It was just kind of a grab bag. They didn't know what they were taking. It was a bad mistake."[22]

Oxycodone as a Gateway Drug

Increasingly often, young people who have never taken any other illegal drug are tempted to try a prescription drug such as oxycodone or Oxy-Contin. In fact, prescription drugs are second only to marijuana as the first illegal drug people try. Too often they are not the last. Experts worry that Percocet, OxyContin, or other oxycodone products may serve as gateway drugs to abuse of other dangerous and illegal drugs, most notably heroin. Amy Caruso of Carlisle, Massachusetts, is but one of thousands of OxyContin addicts who went on to use heroin. At just 20 years old, after months of trying to quit her habit, Caruso died of a drug overdose.

Caruso's story is not unique. The NDIC warns that some oxycodone abusers switch to heroin "as they build tolerance to prescription opioids and seek a more euphoric high."[23] If the supply of oxycodone is compromised, heroin sometimes becomes a replacement. Opioid users may also be tempted by heroin's less expensive price. Oxycodone abusers may spend upward of $400 a day to feed their addiction; getting and staying high on heroin would cost just one-third to one-half of this price. Experts are concerned that the OxyContin epidemic may thereby fuel an increase in heroin abuse.

An increasing number of law enforcement agencies see the problem of prescription drugs as their most serious drug problem. Using many of the same strategies as for illegal street drugs, police are trying to stem the tide of illegal oxycodone products. But addressing prescription drug abuse has proved to be perhaps even more challenging than the entrenched illegal drugs because of their status as a legal drug. Addressing abuse and the spiraling rates of death resulting from this abuse will require a collaborative effort on the part of law enforcement, the medical community, antidrug advocates, and treatment providers.

Primary Source Quotes*

What Are the Health Dangers of Oxycodone Abuse?

"When oxycodone is used for a long time, it may become habit-forming, causing mental or physical dependence."

—Mayo Clinic, "Oxycodone and Acetaminophen," February 1, 2011. www.mayoclinic.com.

The Mayo Clinic is a nonprofit worldwide leader in medical care, research, and education for people from all walks of life.

"While the rates of OxyContin use have increased since 2000, the proportion of those individuals who are prescribed OxyContin and have shown signs of abuse or dependence are quite low (less than 2%)."

—Deni Carise et al., "Prescription OxyContin Abuse Among Patients Entering Addiction Treatment," *American Journal of Psychiatry*, November 2007. http://ajp.psychiatryonline.org.

The authors are researchers in the field of drug abuse and addiction.

Primary Source Quotes

“We are seeing a phenomenal increase in overdose deaths from painkillers—like Oxycontin and Vicodin—often mixed with alcohol. These drugs can kill.”

—Joseph A. Califano Jr., *The Osgood File*, CBS Radio Network, February 8, 2011. www.westwoodone.com.

Califano is founder and chair of the National Center on Addiction and Substance Abuse (CASA) at Columbia University.

“A one-day dose [of prescription pain medication] can be sold on the black market for $100. And a single dose can be lethal to a non-patient. There is no other medicine that has those characteristics.”

—Robert L. DuPont, “Use and Abuse of Prescription Painkillers,” *The Diane Rehm Show*, NPR, April 21, 2011.

A leading expert in drug abuse prevention and treatment, DuPont is currently the president of the Institute for Behavior and Health and served as the first director of the NIDA.

“There are numerous pathways to addiction. Some citizens receive prescriptions for OxyContin for pain after an injury, while adolescents and others experiment with pain medications from medicine cabinets.”

—Steven A. Tolman, “The Deadly Epidemic No One’s Addressing,” *Boston Globe*, May 11, 2009. www.boston.com.

Tolman is a Massachusetts state senator.

“Prescription opioid abusers switch to heroin as they build tolerance to prescription opioids and seek a more euphoric high.”

—NDIC, *National Drug Threat Assessment 2010*, February 2010.

The NDIC is charged with coordinating and publishing information about illegal drug trafficking in the United States.

❝ We are not seeing people die locally from heroin. We're not seeing people die from crack or hydrocodone. [The overdose] deaths that occur are being primarily related to OxyContin.**❞**

—Charles Horner, "Use and Abuse of Prescription Painkillers," *The Diane Rehm Show*, NPR, April 21, 2011.

Horner is the police chief of Portsmouth, Ohio, where fatal drug overdoses have quadrupled in just a few years.

❝ Reducing deaths from opioid overdoses is challenging because such deaths stem from multiple factors, including providers' inappropriate prescribing or inadequate counseling and monitoring, patients' misuse or abuse of drugs, sharing of pain pills with relatives or friends, 'doctor shopping' to obtain multiple prescriptions, and diversion of opioids leading to illicit sales and abuse.**❞**

—Susan Okie, "A Flood of Opioids, a Rising Tide of Deaths," *New England Journal of Medicine*, November 18, 2010.

Okie is a medical journalist and a clinical assistant professor of family medicine at Georgetown University School of Medicine.

What Are the Health Dangers of Oxycodone Abuse?

- Data from the Drug Abuse Warning Network (DAWN) show that **971,914** Americans visited a hospital emergency department for non-medical use of prescription or over-the-counter medications in 2008.

- Statistics from DAWN show that **57,335** men and **47,873** women sought emergency room treatment for abuse of oxycodone in 2008.

- Emergency department visits involving the nonmedical use of oxycodone products increased **152 percent** between 2004 and 2008 (the latest year for which statistics are available).

- According to the CDC, the number of deaths from accidental overdose on opioid pain relievers almost doubled between 2002 **(5,547 deaths)** and 2006 **(11,001 deaths)**.

- Nonmedical use of prescription drugs is the nation's second leading cause of **accidental death**—following automobile accidents—according to data from the CDC.

- In recent years prescription pain medications have been involved in more overdose deaths than **heroin and cocaine combined**, according to DAWN.

- According to data from the National Survey on Drug Use and Health and the National Comorbidity Survey databases, **one in four** users of opiates will become addicted.

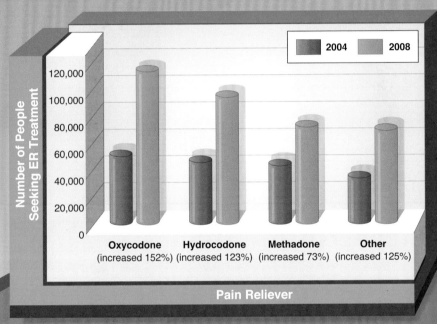

The Rapid Growth of Oxycodone-Related Emergencies

While all opioid pain relievers pose risks, oxycodone appears to be the most dangerous of them all. In 2008 more people sought treatment at an emergency room for nonmedical use of oxycodone than for any other pain reliever. Experts are concerned not only about the sheer number of episodes, but about the rapid increase. Between 2004 and 2008, the number of people seeking emergency department treatment for oxycodone abuse increased 152 percent.

Source: Substance Abuse and Mental Health Services Administration, *The DAWN Report: Trends in Emergency Department Visits Involving Nonmedical Use of Narcotic Pain Relievers*, June 18, 2010.

- In Massachusetts the addiction rate for OxyContin increased by **950 percent** in 10 years, according to the Massachusetts OxyContin and Heroin Commission, which was created to study the problem.

- A study reported in the 2009 issue of *General Hospital Psychiatry* found significantly higher rates of long-term opioid use in patients diagnosed with **depression** than in those without.

Opioid Overdoses on the Rise

The number of people dying from drug overdoses has increased consistently over the past decade, fueled by an increase in addiction to opioid pain relievers. Between 2001 and 2006 the number of people who died from accidental overdose of opioid painkillers more than doubled. Experts say that oxycodone products—especially OxyContin—are responsible for more than 50 percent of these deaths.

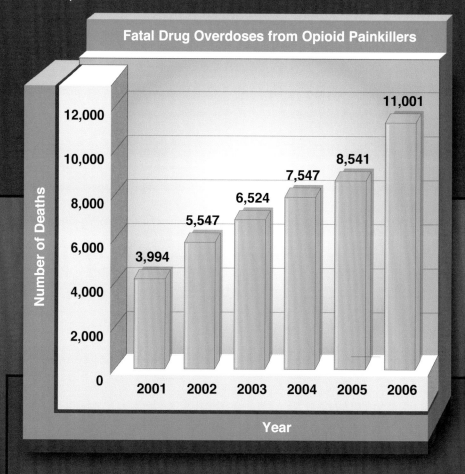

Fatal Drug Overdoses from Opioid Painkillers

Source: National Drug Intelligence Center, *National Drug Threat Assessment 2010*, February 2010.

- The National Survey on Drug Use and Health reveals that **29 percent** of people who used illicit drugs for the first time in 2009 began by using prescription drugs nonmedically.

Opioid Painkillers as a Gateway Drug?

For 17 percent of the US population, illegal drug use began with prescription painkillers. More people took painkillers as their first illegal drug than any other drug except marijuana. Antidrug advocates are concerned that prescription drugs are tempting to first-time users also because people assume these drugs are safer than street drugs. There is some evidence that addicts later turn to other street drugs, particularly heroin.

First Illegal Drug Use

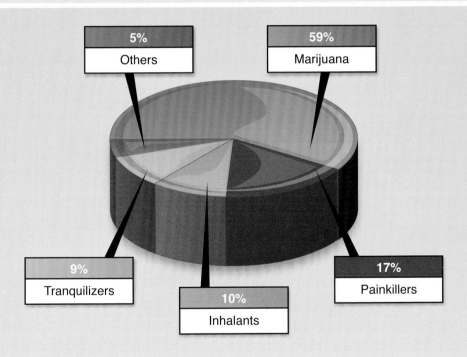

5% Others

59% Marijuana

9% Tranquilizers

10% Inhalants

17% Painkillers

Source: Substance Abuse and Mental Health Services Administration, "Results from the 2009 National Survey on Drug Use and Health: Summary of National Findings," September 2010. http://oas.samhsa.gov.

- In 2008, **19.3 percent** of Americans who went to the emergency room seeking detox or substance abuse treatment services did so for oxycodone.

Should the Government Do More to Control Oxycodone?

> **"While we must ensure better access to prescription drugs to alleviate suffering, it is also vital that we do all we can to curtail dangerous diversion and abuse of pharmaceuticals."**
>
> —Office of National Drug Control Policy (ONDCP), the White House office responsible for setting the nation's drug control policies.

> **"Control of prescription medications needs to involve manufacturers, prescribers, pharmacists, hospitals, state regulators, and consumers in a comprehensive approach for the control of these drugs."**
>
> —Massachusetts OxyContin Commission, a task force charged with addressing that state's OxyContin abuse epidemic.

Government agencies at all levels are involved in the fight against illegal drugs, including prescription narcotics such as oxycodone. Federal agencies—including the FDA, the DEA, and the FBI—have sought ways to reduce the amount of oxycodone available to addicts and abusers. State and local and governments also have engaged in a host of efforts to keep oxycodone off the streets. In addition to enforcing the nation's drug laws, these attempts include monitoring the prescriptions that have been written and passing legislation to shut down pain management clinics that liberally prescribe narcotic pain relievers.

FDA Oversight

The FDA regulates the use of prescription drugs, including oxycodone products. In 2001, in response to growing concerns about addiction and abuse, the FDA required the manufacturer of OxyContin to add a black box warning to its label—the most serious type of warning label. Essentially, the warning tells doctors and consumers that the product carries a high risk of addiction and abuse. "OxyContin contains oxycodone which is an opioid agonist and a Schedule II controlled substance with an abuse liability similar to morphine," the label reads. "All patients receiving opioids should be routinely monitored for signs of misuse, abuse and addiction."[24]

The warning label may help raise awareness among some consumers, but many people believe it falls far short of reducing the risk of abuse. In response to ongoing concerns, in the summer of 2010 the FDA issued a proposal that would have required drug manufacturers to develop guides for physicians on patient selection, dosing, and monitoring of the drugs and patient education guidelines on the safe use and disposal of opioids. The FDA advisory panel reviewing the proposal rejected it because they believed it did not go far enough: They argued that immediate-release opioids (such as hydrocodone) should be included in the plan. The advisory group also suggested that physicians prescribing opioids should be required to take continuing medical education courses—a requirement that some say is infeasible, given the number of doctors who would be affected by the law.

> " In April 2011 the FDA approved a new form of OxyContin. The new pills have a plastic coating designed to prevent them from being cut, broken, chewed, or crushed. "

FDA oversight also led to charges against Purdue Pharma, the manufacturer of OxyContin. In 2007 three former executives from Purdue Pharma pleaded guilty to criminal charges that the company had misled doctors and patients when it claimed the drug was less likely to be abused than traditional narcotics. The manufacturer was ordered to pay $634.5 million—the largest penalty ever paid by a drug company in such a case.

Making the Drug Safer

In April 2010 the FDA approved a new form of OxyContin. The new pills have a plastic coating designed to prevent them from being cut, broken, chewed, or crushed, but experts caution that the new form can still be abused by simply ingesting larger doses than prescribed.

With FDA approval came a requirement that manufacturer Purdue Pharma collect data on the extent to which the new formulation reduces abuse and misuse of this opioid. New rules will also require the drug manufacturer to develop educational programs for patients and prescribers.

The Supply Chain

State and local law enforcement agencies often play a key role in addressing illegal oxycodone use and distribution. For instance, in October 2009 Kentucky State Police detectives and troopers worked with the FBI in Operation Flamingo Road. The sting targeted drug dealers who had traveled to southern Florida to obtain oxycodone from pain clinic doctors and returned to Kentucky to illegally distribute the drugs.

> One of the obstacles to addressing the supply of prescription drugs like oxycodone is that neither buyers nor sellers are 'typical' users and drug dealers.

Florida has become a hotbed for the illegal oxycodone trade. In the first six months of 2010, doctors in Florida prescribed nine times more oxycodone than was sold in the entire United States. The largest problem is in southern Florida, where more than 500 pain clinics in just three counties (Broward, Palm Beach, and Miami-Dade) churn out prescription drugs to walk-in patients.

The effect reaches far beyond Florida. According to the state's Prescription Drug Monitoring Program, "Florida has become the epicenter for the availability of controlled prescription drugs; not only Floridians but out-of-state seekers of the easily obtained controlled substances flock to Florida thereby establishing the 'Flamingo Express.'"[25]

The Suburban Supply

One of the obstacles to addressing the supply of prescription drugs like oxycodone is that buyers and sellers often do not fit the profile of the "typical" users and drug dealers. Many users are professionals who rely on increasing numbers of pills just to make it through the day. Their dealers are not gang members, but doctors or even housewives. For instance, in 2010 Donna M. George was convicted of selling Percocet, methadone, and oxycodone while babysitting for her three young grandchildren in her home in a gated community of suburban Fredericksburg, Virginia.

The federal government has responded with an interagency investigation that it calls Operation Cotton Candy. Despite thousands of arrests of people like George, law enforcement officials say the trafficking continues. "We're seeing remarkable increases in Percocets sold on the street," said Deputy Cuno Andersen, a deputy in the Loudon County, Virginia, sheriff's office and a member of the Cotton Candy task force. "Oxy is off the charts."[26]

Targeting Pill Mills

Federal and state law enforcement officers have targeted pill mills—the doctors and clinics that churn out painkillers and prescriptions without adequately assessing needs. In November 2009, for instance, federal law officials targeted a prescription drug trafficking ring that had operated in southern Florida for three years. The drug ring shipped thousands of oxycodone pills per day by overnight delivery to abusers as far away as Kentucky, North Carolina, Tennessee, Virginia, and West Virginia. In February 2011 state and federal agents raided six pain clinics in southern Florida that dispensed oxycodone to patients recruited via the Internet. Six clinic owners and operators were indicted on charges they conspired to illegally dispense more than 660,000 doses of oxycodone, netting $22 million in profits. According to the indictment:

> The defendants marketed the clinics through more than 1,600 internet sites, required immediate cash payments from patients for a clinic "visit fee," directed the patients

to obtain MRIs that the defendants knew to be inferior, over-aggressively interpreted MRIs in order to justify prescriptions, and falsified patients' urine tests for a fee to justify the highly addictive pain medications.[27]

The DEA reports that this is but one group of arrests stemming from Operation Pill Nation, in which federal, state, and local law enforcement officers have worked together to address the illegal pill mills in southern Florida. In just one year, undercover officers illegally bought more than 340 prescription drugs from over 60 doctors in more than 40 such pill mills.

Of course, Florida is not the only place where doctors have been involved in the illegal distribution of prescription drugs. In May 2008 Masoud Bamdad, a physician in California's San Fernando Valley, was indicted after an 8-month DEA investigation revealed that he was writing prescriptions for oxycodone to people whom he had not examined. Bamdad allegedly charged $100 to $300 for each prescription, generating an average of $30,000 a week. The volume of his prescriptions exceeded that of many hospitals and pain management clinics.

Addressing Theft and Fraud

While federal agents have led investigations into oxycodone rings that cross state boundaries, local law enforcement officers have been charged with addressing local crimes, including armed robberies of pharmacies. As the problem has grown, pharmacies, too, have sought to protect themselves. Some pharmacies have chosen not to stock any oxycodone products, while others have limited their supply to what might be needed by real patients on any given day. Many pharmacies have stepped up their surveillance and protection measures while also training pharmacy personnel on how to handle robberies.

In 2004 several pharmacies joined with law enforcement and drug manufacturers to establish RxPatrol, a national database to collect and analyze information that can assist law enforcement investigations of pharmacy crimes. The measure has helped law enforcement officials catch a number of criminals who have targeted pharmacies, but experts worry that the money that can be made from the illegal diversion of oxycodone and other narcotic painkillers may entice new criminals to take their place.

Controlling oxycodone also involves addressing fraudulent prescriptions. Several states have implemented programs requiring tamper-resistant prescription pads. New York, for instance, requires that all prescriptions for controlled substances be written on official New York State prescription pads, which contain tamper-resistant features. Tamper-resistant prescription pads are also required by the federal government in order for Medicaid to reimburse patients and states for the cost of prescription drugs.

Prescription Drug Monitoring Programs

Because much of the oxycodone that hits the street is sold by pharmacies to people with valid prescriptions, interrupting the supply requires additional oversight at the pharmacy level. Many larger pharmacies have databases that allow pharmacists to access a patient's prescription drug history. Because the databases of different pharmacies are not interconnected, however, patients can sometimes avoid detection by having prescriptions filled at several places.

States are addressing the problem with drug monitoring programs that cross-reference patients, drugs, and prescribing doctors. Monitoring programs enable health care practitioners to view a patient's prescription drug history to find duplicative prescriptions and determine whether the patient has seen multiple physicians for the same prescription. Thirty-eight states currently have programs in place, and most of the others are considering implementing such programs.

Studies have shown that the presence of a prescription drug monitoring program reduces the per capita supply of prescription pain relievers, reducing the probability of abuse for these drugs, but its impact depends

> " Monitoring programs enable health care practitioners to view a patient's prescription drug history to find duplicative prescriptions and determine whether the patient has seen multiple physicians for the same prescription. "

on the extent of the program and the accuracy of the data. In many states the monitoring systems provide reactive information, so doctors or pharmacists first learn that a patient has had a prescription filled elsewhere weeks after seeing the patient. Some states have sought to strengthen the programs by requiring doctors and pharmacists to access patient information in the database before prescribing or dispensing a drug such as oxycodone, but most such proposals have been shot down because they would be too cumbersome for users.

> " Massachusetts is among the states that have called for moving oxycodone from a Schedule II to a Schedule I drug, the class reserved for illegal street drugs such as heroin, cocaine, and marijuana. "

Prescription monitoring systems have critics. Some people believe they invade the privacy of patients, particularly when users beyond the medical community—such as law enforcement officials—have access. They also can be expensive, and some states have included them in recent budget cuts. In 2005 Congress enacted the National All Schedules Prescription Electronic Reporting Act, authorizing a system of federally supported, state-based drug monitoring programs. The program is intended to build on the state-run monitoring programs and provide a more cohesive and streamlined way to detect when patients are getting prescriptions from more than one doctor. Antidrug advocates and physicians say this could provide an invaluable preventive tool, but it has yet to be funded.

Strengthening Laws

To deal with the growing numbers of people addicted to oxycodone, states have passed laws strengthening oversight measures for prescription painkillers. For example, a Washington State law went into effect in 2011 to require additional training for doctors and nurse practitioners who prescribe painkillers. Doctors also are required to consult a pain specialist if a patient's opioid dose increases above a certain level without improvement. While some doctors and patient advocates are concerned that such tough measures will make it difficult for patients to access much-needed pain medication, legislators defend the measure as a necessary step in reducing the serious cases of—and deaths from—the liberal use of narcotics.

States also have called for more stringent rules for prescription painkillers in general and/or oxycodone and OxyContin in particular. Massachusetts is among the states that have called for moving oxycodone from a Schedule II to a Schedule I drug, the class reserved for illegal street drugs such as heroin, cocaine, and marijuana. Some people have gone further in the attempt to address the deaths and destruction that OxyContin abuse has left in its wake, demanding the removal of OxyContin from the market. At the BanOxycontin.com website, for instance, people can sign a petition asking for the drug to be removed from the market. "OxyContin is a 'virus' that started an epidemic of addiction and death that has now infected every community in America," the petition reads. "It is time for the FDA to remove the newest substitute for heroin, OxyContin, from the marketplace."[28]

While OxyContin is a target for such measures, given the number of people who benefit from oxycodone products, it is unlikely that all oxycodone products will be pulled from the market. Reducing abuse will continue to depend on strong measures to reduce demand as well as supply of the drug.

Should the Government Do More to Control Oxycodone?

Primary Source Quotes

❝Rogue doctors who run [pill mills] violate their professional oaths and are, in fact, drug dealers. Florida today is 'ground zero' in the fight against pill mills, and we are determined to continue to aggressively pursue those who are responsible for this nationwide epidemic.❞

—Michele M. Leonhart, "DEA-Led Operation Pill Nation Targets Rogue Pain Clinics in South Florida," news release, DEA, February 24, 2011. www.justice.gov.

Leonhart is the administrator of the DEA.

❝In attempt to point the finger, 'pain management specialists' have received increased scrutiny from federal authorities and the media in recent years. . . . But convictions are sporadic at best, and in most cases, careless doctors receive a slap on the wrist rather than jail time.❞

—Dana Owens, "Watchdog Editorial: Severe Penalties, Strict Rules for Doctors Needed to Curb Prescription Abuse Epidemic," Oxy Watchdog, March 21, 2011. http://oxywatchdog.com.

Owens is assistant editor of Oxy Watchdog, a website that seeks to rid America of OxyContin.

* Editor's Note: While the definition of a primary source can be narrowly or broadly defined, for the purposes of Compact Research, a primary source consists of: 1) results of original research presented by an organization or researcher; 2) eyewitness accounts of events, personal experience, or work experience; 3) first-person editorials offering pundits' opinions; 4) government officials presenting political plans and/or policies; 5) representatives of organizations presenting testimony or policy.

❝The problem is, we can't treat pill addiction or dependence like any other type of drug addiction. These are medicines that help people and *must* be available to those in need, so simply going after the drug manufacturers won't work, unless it's to strengthen security measures.❞

—Joshua Lyon, *Pill Head: The Secret Life of a Painkiller Addict*. New York: Hyperion, 2009.

A journalist, Lyon bought his first prescription painkillers on assignment for *Jane* magazine and soon found himself fighting an addiction to the drugs.

❝We have a war going within our own borders, and it's coming out of pharmacies, doctor's offices, [and] pill mills making a profit from selling poison to our citizens. The people who are in this opiate drug ring activity are smart people. They hire the best lawyers, they move the crooked doctors around the country, they have many, many techniques that are used to evade law enforcement.❞

—John Kasich, "Hillbilly Heroin," *Intervention*, A&E, April 10, 2011.

Kasich is the governor of Ohio.

❝Doctors that prescribe more than a 3–4 day prescription at a time for most operations need to be held accountable for patients becoming addicted to [OxyContin]. When the doctors start losing their licenses and ability to practice, losing their lifestyles will result in more control over this drug.❞

—Rob, "Oxycontin Addiction, Abuse and Treatment," Addiction Search, October 31, 2010. www.addictionsearch.com.

Rob's son was addicted to OxyContin for several years before enrolling in a treatment program.

66 On occasion, overly-sensationalized stories of investigation of doctors have hit the nightly news. . . . The consequence is extreme, and not what law enforcement would ever seek—our parents and other loved ones who are in pain simply cannot get the medicines they need. 99

—William Colby, "Balance, Uniformity and Fairness: Effective Strategies for Law Enforcement for Investigating and Prosecuting the Diversion of Prescription Pain Medications While Protecting Appropriate Medical Practice," Center for Practical Bioethics, September 2009. www.practicalbioethics.org.

Colby is a lawyer with the Center for Practical Bioethics.

66 One of the most efficient ways at the state level to stop fraud, and reduce the availability of dangerous prescription drugs, is an active and effective Prescription Monitoring Program. 99

—Commonwealth of Massachusetts, *Recommendations of the OxyContin and Heroin Commission*, November 2009.

The Massachusetts OxyContin and Heroin Commission was formed in 2008 to make recommendations about how to address the prescription drug epidemic in that state.

66 Physicians who appropriately prescribe and/or administer controlled substances to relieve intractable pain should not be subject to the burdens of excessive regulatory scrutiny, inappropriate disciplinary action, or criminal prosecution. 99

—AMA, "About the AMA Position on Pain Management Using Opioid Analgesics," 2010. www.ama-assn.org.

The AMA is the leading professional association of US physicians.

Should the Government Do More to Control Oxycodone?

- The National Center for Health Statistics estimates that **76.5 million** Americans suffer from chronic pain. Studies show that prolonged pain costs businesses millions of dollars in lost productivity.

- According to the DEA, the amount of prescription opioids dispensed through retail pharmacies increased **52 percent** from 2005 to 2009.

- According to the DEA and National Survey on Drug Use and Health data, opioid pain relievers are the most **commonly diverted** prescription drugs.

- Retail pharmacies dispense roughly **257 million** opioid prescriptions a year. In 2008, 50.1 million oxycodone prescriptions were dispensed, according to IMS Health.

- The *New York Times* reported in February 2011 that more than **1,800 pharmacy robberies** had taken place nationally over the last three years, typically conducted by young men seeking opioid painkillers and other drugs.

- The price of OxyContin varies from one community to another, but the DEA estimates that the average street value is about **$1 per milligram**.

Prescription Drug Threat Increasing for Law Enforcement

Controlled prescription drugs are drugs such as oxycodone that are at risk of being diverted for recreational use. OxyContin is the most widely used and dangerous drug within this category. In 2009 almost one in 10 agencies ranked controlled prescription drugs as their greatest drug threat—before street drugs such as heroin, marijuana, and crystal meth. The threat of controlled prescription drugs has grown rapidly in just five years.

Percentage of State and Local Law Enforcement Agencies Reporting Prescription Drugs as Their Greatest Drug Threat, 2005–2009

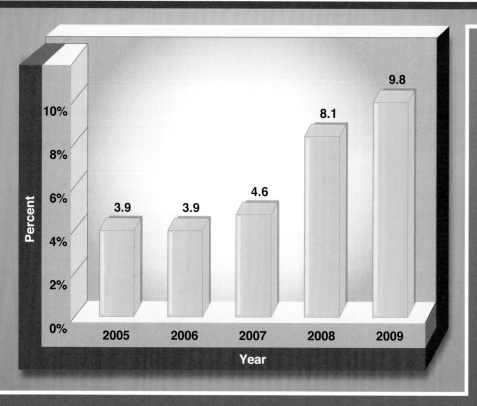

Source: National Drug Intelligence Center, *National Drug Threat Assessment 2010*, February 2010. www.justice.gov.

- In 2009, **48 percent** of state and local law enforcement agencies reported that street gangs were involved in the distribution of prescription drugs, according to the NDIC.

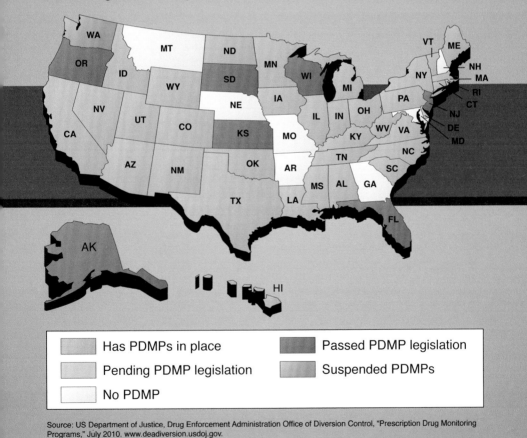

States Add Prescription Drug Monitoring Programs (PDMPs)

Prescription drug monitoring programs that provide a searchable database of prescriptions filled by pharmacies have become a critical tool in the fight against the diversion of oxycodone and other prescription drugs. As of July 2010, 34 states had prescription monitoring programs in place, and 7 additional states had passed legislation to create the programs. Several other states have legislation pending. Washington State had a prescription monitoring program for several years, but it was suspended at the beginning of 2010 because of budgetary constraints. The federal government has enacted legislation to help states finance these programs.

Has PDMPs in place

Passed PDMP legislation

Pending PDMP legislation

Suspended PDMPs

No PDMP

Source: US Department of Justice, Drug Enforcement Administration Office of Diversion Control, "Prescription Drug Monitoring Programs," July 2010. www.deadiversion.usdoj.gov.

- According to the DEA, of the top 100 practitioners that dispense oxycodone from their offices, 96 of them are in **Florida**, and 86 are in a three-county area in southern Florida.

How Can Oxycodone Abuse Be Prevented?

"We must abandon the notion that abuse of controlled prescription drugs like OxyContin . . . is somehow safer than abuse of illegal street drugs."

—Joseph A. Califano Jr., founder and chair of CASA.

"Increased efforts are needed to educate the public about the risks of misusing narcotic pain relievers and how to recognize possible symptoms of abuse."

—SAMHSA, the federal government agency charged with reducing the impact of substance abuse.

In addition to addressing the supply of oxycodone, preventing abuse depends on addressing demand for the drug. As with other drugs, prevention programs include education and awareness for patients who are prescribed drugs containing oxycodone, as well as for others who might be tempted to use the drugs without a prescription. Among other things, this means properly disposing of leftover oxycodone before it makes its way into the hands of teens or other abusers. "Availability and access, we know, leads to misuse. These drugs are there for the taking in medicine cabinets across the country,"[29] says Susan E. Foster, vice president of policy research and analysis at CASA.

Prescription drugs are commonly abused by teens—second only to marijuana—and rival marijuana as the first illegal drug tried by teens.

Recognizing the particular risk to adolescents, a range of programs have been developed targeting children and young adults.

Research indicates that drug use is linked to the perception of risk. Students often assume that prescription drugs like OxyContin provide a safe way for them to get a high. Effective programs demonstrate the serious dangers of using these drugs without a prescription. Some antidrug programs provide real stories of teens whose lives have been changed—or even cut short—by addiction to opiates.

Effective antidrug programs go beyond simple scare tactics, however. The best programs, say experts, address the many reasons that teens become involved with drugs, providing life skills and social skills training that teaches students how to deal with stress and peer pressure and that builds self-esteem. Programs facilitated by individuals other than teachers tend to be more effective. In school-based antidrug programs, peers often play a particularly important role as mentors or role models.

Research also shows that school-based antidrug programs can have a greater impact when they are combined with media and community programs. Media campaigns reinforce school-based prevention programs by reaching youth through popular television shows, Internet sites, magazines, and films. Antidrug media campaigns include a variety of media to communicate the dangers of drug use, including public service announcements, posters and print advertisements, brochures on the dangers of drug abuse, web-based testimonials, and the like.

> **The best programs, say experts, address the many reasons that teens become involved with drugs, providing life skills and social skills training that teaches students how to deal with stress and peer pressure and that builds self-esteem.**

Some antidrug advocates emphasize the importance of addressing the root causes of drug abuse or things that put teens at greater risk of using drugs, such as dropping out of school and involvement in gangs or criminal activity. Because low self-esteem tends to result in a greater desire to conform to what is considered popular or cool, many drug prevention programs attempt to improve students' self-esteem and identify ways in which teens can succeed. Research also suggests that programs that teach life skills are more effective. Young people need to develop the ability to cope with challenges by making informed, mature decisions.

Community-Based Programs

Effective drug resistance programs often include a community focus. For instance, the National Youth Anti-Drug Media Campaign's Above the Influence program delivers drug prevention messages at the national level and through more targeted efforts at the local community level. The ONDCP also oversees the Drug Free Communities program, which was funded initially by Congress in 1997 in recognition of the fact that local problems need local solutions.

> " Parents who would be appalled at the notion of their child trying heroin often do not recognize that OxyContin can be just as deadly. "

Many of these programs have begun to target prescription drugs in general and OxyContin specifically. In response to the disproportionate abuse of OxyContin in East Boston, Massachusetts, in 2011, public health workers were preparing to knock on every door in East Boston with information on the prevention and treatment of drug abuse.

The Role of Physicians

Doctors who prescribe opioids play a key role in the prevention of the abuse. "Anyone who treats pain confronts a balancing act," says Ellen Battista, the director of Pain Treatment Consultants of Western New York. "They have an ethical, moral and professional obligation to treat it. They also must be ethically, morally and professionally concerned about drug addiction and diversion."[30]

Experts say that doctors should be the first line of defense against oxycodone abuse. "As a first step, physicians need to ask questions about a patient's history of addiction or previous difficulties in controlling their prescription drug use,"[31] says the AMA. Physicians also can help reduce the risk of abuse by prescribing a few pills at a time and monitoring closely any patients who have been prescribed an oxycodone product.

Physicians may also play a key role in educating adults about the risk prescription drugs may pose for other members of their family. Advising patients to lock up their medications and providing information about safe disposal of unused drugs may help prevent drugs from falling into the hands of teens.

The Pain Contract

Pain contracts are becoming increasingly common. Some doctors require patients to sign a form declaring that they will get any and all pain medications from one doctor and agreeing to submit to drug testing during the course of their treatment.

Many patients complain that they are being treated like drug addicts, but some experts believe that the contracts give doctors a much-needed tool for recognizing when drugs are being abused. Kevin B. O'Reilly, a staff writer for the AMA, writes, "Many doctors, who are concerned about the high-profile prosecutions of physicians treating patients with chronic pain, use the documents as a way to protect themselves legally while making clear to patients that they will not tolerate diversion."[32]

> " Because many oxycodone addicts become addicted when legitimately prescribed the drug to address a real need, treatment programs to help people get off and stay off the drug are an important aspect of any prevention initiative. "

In 2009 the American Pain Society and the American Academy of Pain Medicine issued guidelines calling for close monitoring of patients prescribed opioid medications, particularly patients who may be at high risk of addiction or abuse. Among the measures recommended is that doctors perform a urine drug screen for patients on opioids. The AMA reports: "Between 21% and 44% of patients who demonstrate no red-flag behaviors [are not considered high risk] have unexpected results on urine drug tests. . . . An additional 7.5% of patients test negative for the opioid drug they are prescribed."[33] Some proponents of drug testing say that a negative test can identify situations in which the drug is being given away or sold to someone else.

The Role of Parents and Families

Research consistently demonstrates that parents can—and do—play an important role in keeping their children drug free. Joseph A. Califano Jr., founder and chair of CASA, says, "Our surveys have consistently found that the more often children have dinners with their parents, the less likely they are to smoke, drink or use drugs, and that parental engagement fostered around the dinner table is one of the most potent tools to help parents raise healthy, drug-free children."[34]

Like young people, many parents underestimate the risks posed by oxycodone and other prescription drugs. Parents who would be appalled at the notion of their child trying heroin often do not recognize that OxyContin can be just as deadly. After Brett Tozzo died of an overdose of OxyContin, alcohol, and heroin, his mother admitted, "Even when he told me he was addicted to painkillers, I still wasn't worried because it wasn't an 'illegal' drug. I was very naïve."[35]

Prescription Drug Take-Back Programs

Unfortunately, many parents fail to lock up dangerous prescription drugs. Not only do teens sometimes raid their parents' medicine cabinet, a friend or visitor may do the same. "Patients tell me they worked as a maid at the height of their addiction and they would go through people's medicine cabinets," says Kyle Kampman, the medical director for an addiction treatment facility. "I had a patient who was a roofer tell me, 'If you ever let a roofer in your house and in the bathroom, chances are they are looking through your medicine cabinet.'"[36]

"That explains it," adds Linda Bourque. "I was prescribed Percocet and Vicodin after an accident. I didn't like the drugs and didn't finish either prescription. When I looked in my drawer a month or two later, there was one empty bottle. The other bottle and the pills remaining on the prescription were gone. We had construction being done on our house, so any number of people could have taken it."[37]

To counter this problem, the federal government launched a campaign to have people dispose of leftover prescription drugs safely. Several local and state governments have launched prescription drug take-back programs to collect drugs remaining on prescriptions. For instance, in Broward County, Florida, home to some of the highest-prescribing doctors of oxycodone, law enforcement officers held their first Operation Medicine Cabinet program in 2008. On September 25, 2010, led by the DEA, the federal government sponsored the first nationwide prescription drug take-back day. In 2008, Maine established a year-round prescription drug take-back program using the mail system. Maine pharmacies provide postage-free envelopes in which consumers can mail unused drugs back to state drug enforcement officials for proper disposal.

On blogs and at treatment centers, former addicts share their stories of recovery. Their advice is the same: Do not start.

The purpose of prescription take-back programs is to provide a venue for people to safely dispose of unwanted and unused prescription drugs. Program leaders say that the widely publicized take-back programs also help to educate Americans about the dangers of storing these drugs at home and provide them with tips for safe disposal.

Treatment as a Prevention Strategy

Because many oxycodone addicts become addicted when legitimately prescribed the drug to address a real need, treatment programs to help people get off and stay off the drug are an important aspect of any prevention initiative. A number of rehabilitation facilities specializing in Oxy-Contin abuse have opened to meet the unique needs of oxycodone addicts. California, for instance, has more than a dozen such rehab centers.

Treatment programs for oxycodone are based on what has worked for heroin addiction. Programs generally include detoxification, in which the user is slowly weaned off the drug, as well as cognitive and/or behavioral therapy intended to address underlying causes of drug use.

Detoxification of OxyContin is a gradual process due to the drug's long-lasting properties. The first stage may involve switching to a shorter-acting opiate such as hydrocodone (Vicodin) for five to seven days, and then to buprenorphine (Suboxone), an opiate that provides relief from pain and anxiety without the euphoria and cravings of these other opiates. Suboxone is usually given for several weeks or even a few months, with the dosage gradually tapering off.

One of the problems with prescribing drugs to treat oxycodone addiction is that users sometimes simply replace oxycodone with another drug, becoming just as dependent on methadone or some other drug. For this reason, experts suggest that drug treatment be part of an intense, highly supervised program and that users be off all drugs before being released. In addition, some experts recommend prescribing sleeping pills, antidepressants, and/or other mood stabilizing medications during recovery.

Many addicts also find help through groups such as Narcotics Anonymous, a support group that grew out of Alcoholics Anonymous in the 1950s. Other websites provide forums for addicts and former addicts. On a multitude of sites, current and past users of OxyContin ask for advice about how to quit and stay off oxycodone and offer support for one another during the long road to recovery.

A Word to the Wise

Given the wide range of reasons that people become tempted by and addicted to oxycodone, antidrug strategies need to be adapted to effectively reach different parts of the community. Oxycodone needs to be an integral part of drug prevention programs designed for teens before they are first tempted to take a drug. Prevention programs also need to convince hardened addicts that giving up the drug is worth the pain and effort and support them on the long road to recovery.

While oxycodone has earned the name "hillbilly heroin," addiction does not discriminate by age, gender, race, or socioeconomic status. On blogs and at treatment centers, former addicts share their stories of recovery. Their advice is the same: Do not start. Parents who have lost children to addiction plead with others to watch for warning signs in their loved ones. Addicts plead with their loved ones to get them help. Those who have lived through the oxycodone epidemic echo the warnings of antidrug experts that oxycodone abuse is inherently dangerous—perhaps even more so than heroin and other street drugs.

How Can Oxycodone Abuse Be Prevented?

> **"The best solution is to reach young people with effective, fact-based drug education—before they start experimenting with drugs. Tweens, teens and young adults who know the facts about drugs are much less likely to start using them."**

—Foundation for a Drug-Free World, "Effective Drug Education Tools for All Teachers and Educators," 2011. www.drugfreeworld.org.

The Foundation for a Drug-Free World is a nonprofit corporation dedicated to the prevention of drug use.

> **"Although many drug education programs have increased knowledge and produced significant attitude changes, traditional drug education programs have not proved to be effective. Information alone does not alter behavior."**

—Raymond Goldberg, *Drugs Across the Spectrum*, 6th ed. Belmont, CA: Wadsworth, 2010.

Goldberg is the dean of health sciences at Vance-Granville Community College in North Carolina.

Bracketed quotes indicate conflicting positions.

* Editor's Note: While the definition of a primary source can be narrowly or broadly defined, for the purposes of Compact Research, a primary source consists of: 1) results of original research presented by an organization or researcher; 2) eyewitness accounts of events, personal experience, or work experience; 3) first-person editorials offering pundits' opinions; 4) government officials presenting political plans and/or policies; 5) representatives of organizations presenting testimony or policy.

Primary Source Quotes

“The popularity of prescription drugs in the street market [is] rooted in the abusers' perceptions of these drugs as less stigmatizing, less dangerous; and less subject to legal consequences than illicit drugs.”

—James A. Inciardi et al., "Prescription Opioid Abuse and Diversion in an Urban Community: The Results of an Ultrarapid Assessment," *Pain Medicine*, April 2009. http://onlinelibrary.wiley.com.

The authors are leading researchers in the field of pain management and medicine.

“Ignorance about the dangers of some of these drugs—and the availability of them, despite some controls over the prescription—are why this country has such an ongoing and increasing epidemic of deaths from opiates.”

—Sidney Wolfe, *The Osgood File*, CBS Radio Network, February 8, 2011. www.westwoodone.com.

Wolfe is the cofounder and director of the Public Citizen's Health Research Group, which was formed to protect consumers by advocating stronger physician accountability and safer drugs.

“Ongoing efforts are needed to keep doctors and other health care professionals informed about emerging drug problems and to help them understand the importance of exercising care in prescribing pain relievers and monitoring their patients or clients for signs of misuse.”

—SAMHSA, *DAWN Report*, June 18, 2010.

A federal agency, SAMHSA funds and administers a wide range of programs to address substance abuse among Americans.

“Some individuals who abuse prescription drugs, particularly teens, believe these substances are safer than illicit drugs because they are prescribed by a health-care professional.”

—ONDCP, "Prescription Drugs: Weighing the Benefits and the Risks," fact sheet, December 2010.

The ONDCP is the White House office responsible for establishing and directing US drug policies.

66 Prevention should be 'laser beamed' on children. Sixteen years of research at The National Center on Addiction and Substance Abuse finds that a child who gets through age 21 without smoking, using illegal drugs, or abusing alcohol is virtually certain never to do so. 99

—Joseph A. Califano Jr., "High Society: How Substance Abuse Ravages America and What to Do About It," *On the Brain*, Fall 2008.

Califano is the founder and chair of CASA.

··

66 Quality, evidence-based drug education in schools and well-designed after-school activities can reduce the risk that teens will get into drugs, but parents remain the first line of defense. 99

—ONDCP, "Back to School: Helping Kids Lead Healthy, Safe, and Drug-Free Lives," *ONDCP Update*, August/September, 2010.

The ONDCP is the White House office responsible for establishing and directing US drug policies.

··

66 Some parents become 'passive pushers' by leaving around the house addictive prescription drugs like OxyContin and Vicodin, making them easily available to their children. 99

—Joseph A. Califano Jr., "Accompanying Statement of Joseph A. Califano, Jr. on National Survey of American Attitudes on Substance Abuse XIII: Teens and Parents," August 14, 2008. www.casacolumbia.org.

Califano is the founder and chair of CASA.

··

How Can Oxycodone Abuse Be Prevented?

- Education of patients may help reduce the rate of oxycodone addiction and abuse. In a MediGuard poll of oxycodone users, **20 percent** of patients said they wished they had been told more before they started taking oxycodone.

- In a 2010 study undertaken by CASA, nearly **one in five** teens said they could illegally obtain prescription drugs in an hour.

- According to the ONDCP, more than **70 percent** of people who misuse prescription pain medications such as OxyContin (oxycodone) and Vicodin (hydrocodone) say they get them from friends or relatives.

- A 2010 study undertaken by the University of Maryland found that **35 percent** of college students who were prescribed pain relievers had sold or given them away at least once.

- The federal government led the first National Prescription Drug Take-Back Day in September 2010. Americans turned in over **242,000 pounds**—121 tons (110 metric tons)—of prescription drugs during this event.

- In a recent survey undertaken by Partnership for a Drug-Free America, **40 percent** of teens agreed that prescription medications are much safer to use than illegal drugs, even if the prescription drugs are not taken as prescribed.

Prescription Pain Relievers Are Too Easy to Get

Preventing drug abuse depends on reducing the supply. Experts warn that narcotic pain relievers are often too readily available to young people. In a new trend, teens search their parents' medicine cabinets for party drugs, such as OxyContin or Percocet. As shown in this chart, high school seniors believe that it is much easier to get opiate pain relievers than any drug other than marijuana. In fact more than 50 percent of twelfth graders say it would be "fairly easy" or "very easy" to get these drugs.

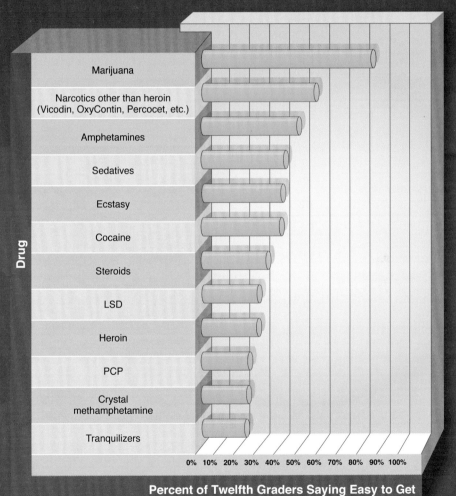

Drug (y-axis):
- Marijuana
- Narcotics other than heroin (Vicodin, OxyContin, Percocet, etc.)
- Amphetamines
- Sedatives
- Ecstasy
- Cocaine
- Steroids
- LSD
- Heroin
- PCP
- Crystal methamphetamine
- Tranquilizers

0% 10% 20% 30% 40% 50% 60% 70% 80% 90% 100%

Percent of Twelfth Graders Saying Easy to Get

Source: Lloyd D. Johnston et al., *Monitoring the Future: National Results on Adolescent Drug Use, 2010*, National Institute on Drug Abuse, February 2011.

How People Get Prescription Painkillers

Because oxycodone products are legal when taken as prescribed, prevention efforts must focus on addressing the diversion from legal to illegal sale and use. Many experts stress that many people get the drugs from a friend or relative. Almost three-quarters (70.2 percent) of people using prescription pain relievers for nonmedical purposes, got them from a friend or relative, whether for free, buying them, or taking them without asking.

Source of Prescription Pain Relievers

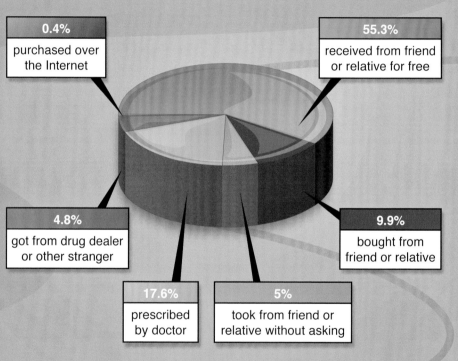

0.4%
purchased over
the Internet

55.3%
received from friend
or relative for free

4.8%
got from drug dealer
or other stranger

9.9%
bought from
friend or relative

17.6%
prescribed
by doctor

5%
took from friend or
relative without asking

Source: Substance Abuse and Mental Health Services Administration, "Results from the 2009 National Survey on Drug Use and Health: Summary of National Findings," September 2010. www.oas.samhsa.gov.

- In a recent survey only **1 percent** of parents of teens said it was "extremely or very likely" that their teen had taken a prescription painkiller, but 21 percent of teens admitted to nonmedical use of prescription painkillers.

An Increasing Number of Americans Seek Help for Opioid Addiction

Because it is so easy to become addicted to oxycodone, experts warn that treating people for their addiction is a critical step in drug prevention efforts. As shown in this graph, the number of people in treatment for pain relievers more than doubled between 2002 and 2009. Researchers estimate that at least half of the people in these treatment programs are addicted to oxycodone.

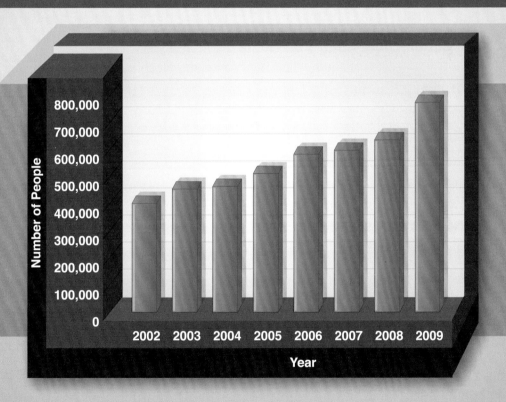

Number of People in Treatment for Opioid Abuse

Source: Substance Abuse and Mental Health Services Administration, "Results from the 2009 National Survey on Drug Use and Health: Summary of National Findings," September 2010. http://oas.samhsa.gov.

• According to a study published in the April/May 2011 issue of the *Clinical Journal of Pain*, Americans spend more than **$2.2 billion** on direct treatment for addiction to prescription opioids.

Key People and Advocacy Groups

American Medical Association (AMA): As the leading professional organization of US physicians, the AMA has offered ongoing commentary on how to balance the need of patients in chronic pain against the need to protect against opioid addiction.

Joseph A. Califano Jr.: Califano is the founder and chair of CASA at Columbia University.

Paul Christo: Christo is director of the Multidisciplinary Pain Fellowship Program at the Johns Hopkins University Hospital and director of its pain treatment center. Christo is among the many pain management specialists who emphasize that the risks of pain relievers must be balanced against the benefits they bring for patients suffering from chronic pain.

Erin Marie Daly: Daly is a journalist who founded Oxy Watchdog, which keeps an eye on news related to OxyContin, following her brother's addiction to OxyContin, subsequent use of heroin, and 2009 death of a heroin overdose.

Drug Free America Foundation: The Drug Free America Foundation is a national drug prevention nonprofit group committed to opposing efforts that would legalize, decriminalize, or promote illicit drugs, including marijuana.

Drug Policy Alliance: The Drug Policy Alliance lobbies for drug reform policy that is grounded in science, compassion, health, and human rights and seeks alternatives to the US government's war on drugs.

Robert L. DuPont: DuPont is the president of the Institute for Behavior and Health and former director of the NIDA. He works to educate the public on dangers of illicit drug use and to lobby for reforms that will address the diversion of prescription drugs without taking them out of the hands of patients who need them.

Gil Kerlikowske: Kerlikowske is the director of the ONDCP, which sets policy for the nation's approach to drug addiction, drug abuse, and illegal drug use.

National Institute on Drug Abuse (NIDA): NIDA is the arm of the US Department of Health and Human Services that supports research into drug abuse and addiction and disseminates the results of this research.

Pain Relief Network: The network was formed in 2003 to oppose the federal government's crackdown on opioid pain relievers by calling attention to the plight of people in chronic pain and their difficulties in finding treatment.

Purdue Pharma: Purdue Pharma is the manufacturer of OxyContin. Company spokespersons believe that OxyContin is safe when used as directed and emphasize that the company has worked with the FDA to improve the safety of the formulation and to educate physicians, patients, and others about drug safety.

Nora Volkow: Volkow is one of the country's foremost addiction researchers and the director of the NIDA. An expert on the brain's dopamine system, Volkow has been instrumental in demonstrating that drug addiction is a disease of the human brain.

Chronology

1938
The Federal Food, Drug, and Cosmetic Act gives the federal government authority to regulate the safety of drugs sold to Americans and leads to the creation of the FDA.

1916
Oxycodone is synthesized at the University of Frankfurt as part of an attempt to improve on existing opioids, such as morphine, heroin, and codeine.

1939
Oxycodone is introduced to the US market.

1910   1940   1970

1931
The League of Nation's Convention for Limiting the Manufacture and Regulating the Distribution of Narcotic Drugs includes oxycodone.

1961
The United Nations includes oxycodone in the list of drugs to be limited for medical and scientific purposes only.

1966
The Narcotic Addict Rehabilitation Act marks a shift from punishment to treatment for "certain persons charged with or convicted of violating Federal Criminal laws, who are determined to be addicted to narcotic drugs, and likely to be rehabilitated through treatment."

1970

The Comprehensive Drug Abuse Prevention and Control Act categorizes drugs based on abuse and addiction potential compared to their therapeutic value.

2011

The ONDCP issues an action plan to address the national prescription drug abuse epidemic; the plan requires drug manufacturers to develop education programs for doctors about the safe use of opioids such as oxycodone.

1976

The FDA approves oxycodone for relief of pain.

2010

In an attempt to address concerns about abuse, Purdue Pharma reformulates OxyContin to lessen the ability to tamper with the opioid medication through cutting, breaking, chewing, crushing, or dissolving it.

1970   1990   2010

1973

Researchers discover that special receptors in the brain are responsible for the effects of opiates; this discovery paves the way for research into ways to block these effects.

1996

Purdue Pharma begins manufacturing OxyContin. By 2001 annual sales in the United States exceed $1 billion, making OxyContin the best-selling narcotic pain reliever in the country.

2001

In response to what is perceived to be a growing epidemic, particularly in rural areas of the United States, the DEA initiates the OxyContin Action Plan, targeting the illegal sale and use of prescription pain relievers.

2007

Purdue Pharma and three of its top executives plead guilty to charges that they misrepresented the dangers of OxyContin abuse.

Related Organizations

American Academy of Pain Medicine (AAPM)

4700 W. Lake Ave.
Glenview, IL 60025
phone: (847) 375-4731 • fax: (847) 375-6477
e-mail: info@painmed.org • website: www.painmed.org

The AAPM is the medical specialty society representing physicians practicing in the field of pain medicine. The academy is involved in education, training, advocacy, and research in the specialty of pain medicine.

American Association for the Treatment of Opioid Dependence (AATOD)

225 Varick St., 4th Floor
New York, NY 10014
phone: (212) 566-5555 • fax: (212) 366-4647
e-mail: info@aatod.org • website: www.aatod.org

The AATOD was founded in 1984 to enhance the quality of patient care in treatment programs by promoting the growth and development of comprehensive methadone treatment services throughout the United States.

American Society of Addiction Medicine (ASAM)

4601 N. Park Ave., Upper Arcade #101
Chevy Chase, MD 20815
phone: (301) 656-3920 • fax: (301) 656-3815
e-mail: email@asam.org • website: www.asam.org

The ASAM is a professional society representing close to 3,000 physicians dedicated to increasing access to and improving the quality of addiction treatment, educating physicians and the public, supporting research and prevention, and promoting the appropriate role of physicians in the care of patients with addictions.

Foundation for a Drug-Free World

1626 N. Wilcox Ave., Suite 1297
Los Angeles, CA 90028
phone: (888) 668-6378
website: www.drugfreeworld.org

The Foundation for a Drug-Free World is a nonprofit corporation that spearheads a multipronged approach to prevent drug use, including public service announcements, educational programs and materials, and web-based outreach.

Narcotics Anonymous

PO Box 999
Van Nuys, CA 91409
phone: (818) 773-9999 • fax: (818) 700-0700
e-mail: fsmail@na.org • website: www.na.org

Based on the approach of Alcoholics Anonymous, Narcotics Anonymous serves as a support group for people addicted to narcotic drugs. The group also publishes periodicals and reports on topics related to drugs and addiction.

National Center on Addiction and Substance Abuse (CASA)

Columbia University
633 Third Ave.
New York, NY 10017
phone: (212) 841-5200
website: www.casacolumbia.org

CASA is a nonprofit organization that brings together the professional disciplines needed to study and combat abuse of all substances, including prescription drugs like oxycodone.

National Institute on Drug Abuse (NIDA)

6001 Executive Blvd., Room 5213
Bethesda, MD 20892
phone: (301) 443-1124
e-mail: information@nida.nih.gov • website: www.nida.nih.gov

The NIDA is part of the National Institutes of Health, a branch of the Department of Health and Human Services. It both supports and conducts extensive scientific research on drug abuse and addiction. By disseminating its research findings, the NIDA hopes to prevent drug abuse, improve treatment options, and influence public policy.

Office of National Drug Control Policy (ONDCP)

PO Box 6000
Rockville, MD 20849
phone: (800) 666-3332 • fax: (301) 519-5212
website: www.whitehousedrugpolicy.gov

The ONDCP was established by the Anti-Drug Abuse Act of 1988 to formulate and implement the nation's drug control program. The goals of the program are to reduce illicit drug use and drug-related trafficking, crime, and violence.

Pain Relief Network

518 Old Santa Fe Trail, Suite #1, Box 519
Santa Fe, NM 87505
phone: (877) 473-5434 • fax: (505) 995-6201
e-mail: info@painreliefnetwork.org • website: http://painreliefnetwork.org

The Pain Relief Network was formed in 2003 to oppose the federal government's crackdown on providers of pain relief. The network ceased its advocacy efforts in 2010, but has continued to maintain its website to provide a resource for patients, families, and physicians seeking pain management and treatment options.

Partnership for a Drug-Free America

405 Lexington Ave., Suite 1601
New York, NY 10174
phone: (212) 922-1560 • fax: (212) 922-1570
website: www.drugfreeamerica.org

The Partnership for a Drug-Free America is a nonprofit organization that works to educate the public, particularly young people, about the dangers of drug abuse. Through extensive media campaigns, the partnership hopes to spread its antidrug message and prevent drug abuse among the nation's youth.

Substance Abuse and Mental Health Services Administration (SAMHSA)

1 Choke Cherry Rd.
Rockville, MD 20857
phone: (877) 726-4727 • fax: (240) 221-4292
website: www.samhsa.gov

This agency of the US Department of Health and Human Services funds and administers a wide range of programs to address substance abuse among Americans. It also collects, analyzes, and disseminates national data on behavioral health practices and issues, including the annual National Survey on Drug Use and Health.

Treatment Research Institute (TRI)

600 Public Ledger Building
150 S. Independence Mall West
Philadelphia, PA 19106
phone: (215) 399-0980
website: www.tresearch.org

The TRI is an independent nonprofit research and development organization dedicated to science-driven reform of treatment and policy in substance abuse.

US Drug Enforcement Administration (DEA)

2401 Jefferson Davis Hwy.
Alexandria, VA 22301
phone: (202) 307-1000
website: www.usdoj.gov/dea

The DEA enforces federal laws that prohibit the trafficking of illegal drugs, including marijuana, and assists state and local law enforcement officers in their efforts to stop illegal drug trafficking and abuse.

For Further Research

Books

Amy E. Breguet and Ronald J. Brogan, *Vicodin, OxyContin, and Other Pain Relievers*. New York: Chelsea House, 2008.

Rod Colvin, *Overcoming Prescription Drug Addiction: A Guide to Coping and Understanding*. Omaha, NE: Addicus, 2008.

Bradley V. DeHaven, *Defining Moments: A Suburban Father's Journey into His Son's Oxy Addiction*. Scotts Valley, CA: CreateSpace, 2011.

David Kipper and Steven Whitney, *The Addiction Solution*. New York: Rodale, 2010.

Joshua Lyon, *Pill Head: The Secret Life of a Painkiller Addict*. New York: Hyperion, 2009.

Marvin Seppala, *Prescription Painkillers: History, Pharmacology, and Treatment*. Center City, MN: Hazelden, 2010.

Todd A. Zalkins, *Dying for Triplicate: A True Story of Addiction, Survival, and Recovery*. Scotts Valley, CA: CreateSpace, 2010.

Internet Sources

American Academy of Pain Medicine, "Pain Medicine Position Paper," 2009. http://onlinelibrary.wiley.com/doi/10.1111/j.1526-4637.2009.00696.x/pdf.

The Henry J. Kaiser Family Foundation, "Prescription Drug Trends," May 2007. www.kff.org/rxdrugs/index.cfm.

Lloyd D. Johnston et al., *Monitoring the Future: National Results on Adolescent Drug Use, 2009*, National Institute on Drug Abuse, May 2010. http://monitoringthefuture.org/pubs/monographs/overview2009.pdf.

National Institute on Drug Abuse, "Facts on Opioids," October 2009. http://teens.drugabuse.gov/peerx/pdf/PEERx_Toolkit_FactSheets_Opioids.pdf.

———, "NIDA InfoFacts: Prescription Pain and Other Medications," July 2009. www.drugabuse.gov/infofacts/PainMed.html.

————, "Prescription Drugs: Abuse and Addiction," August 2005. www.drugabuse.gov/ResearchReports/Prescription/Prescription.html.

Office of National Drug Control Policy, "Drug Facts: Prescription Drugs." www.whitehousedrugpolicy.gov/drugfact/prescrptn_drgs/index.html.

Substance Abuse and Mental Health Services Administration, *Drug Abuse Warning Network, 2007: National Estimates of Drug-Related Emergency Department Visits*, May 2010. https://dawninfo.samhsa.gov/pubs/edpubs.

————, "OxyContin: Prescription Drug Abuse—2008 Revision," *Substance Abuse Treatment Advisory*, Summer 2008. http://store.samhsa.gov/shin/content/SMA08-4138/SMA08-4138.pdf.

USA Today/Kaiser Family Foundation/Harvard School of Public Health, "The Public on Prescription Drugs and Pharmaceutical Companies," March 4, 2008. www.kff.org/kaiserpolls/pomr030408pkg.cfm.

US Food and Drug Administration, "OxyContin: Questions and Answers," April 5, 2010. www.fda.gov/Drugs/DrugSafety/Postmarket DrugSafetyInformationforPatientsandProviders/ucm207196.htm.

Websites

Drug Sense (www.drugsense.org). This site provides a comprehensive index of online news clips about drugs, including oxycodone.

Drug War Facts (www.drugwarfacts.org). This website provides information pertaining to public health and criminal justice issues.

"Drug Wars," *Frontline* (www.pbs.org/wgbh/pages/frontline/shows/drugs). This website, which serves as a companion to the PBS series of reports on the drug war, provides information, interviews, and discussions about America's war on drugs.

NIDA for Teens, National Institute on Drug Abuse (http://teens.drugabuse.gov/facts). This site includes basic information on drug abuse for teens, including definitions, possible short- and long-term side effects, and stories from teen users.

Oxy Watchdog (http://oxywatchdog.com). This site includes news about OxyContin, including the crimes committed on a daily basis, as well as resources, stories of addicts and their families, and reports.

Source Notes

Overview

1. Susan J. Landers, "Dangerous Diversions: Specter of Prescription Drug Abuse Creates Tough Balancing Act for Doctors," *American Medical News*, March 17, 2008. www.ama-assn.org.
2. Quoted in Erin Allday, "Pain Often Under-Treated on Fears of Drug Abuse," *San Francisco Chronicle*, February 19, 2011. http://articles.sfgate.com.
3. Quoted in Landers, "Dangerous Diversions."
4. Quoted in Landers, "Dangerous Diversions."
5. Quoted in Allday, "Pain Often Under-Treated on Fears of Drug Abuse."

How Serious a Problem Is Oxycodone Abuse?

6. Quoted in Steven Goff, "'I Should Have Been Dead': Drug Addiction Nearly Cost United's Quaranta His Career, and More," *Washington Post*, Saturday, June 14, 2008, p. E5.
7. Quoted in Austin News, "'Doctor Shopping' a Growing Crime of Desperation," April 7, 2008. www.kxan.com.
8. Melody Petersen, *Our Daily Meds: How the Pharmaceutical Companies Transformed Themselves into Slick Marketing Machines and Hooked the Nation on Prescription Drugs.* New York: Farrar, Straus and Giroux, 2008, p. 266.
9. Abby Goodnough, "Pharmacies Besieged by Addicted Thieves," *New York Times*, February 6, 2011. www.nytimes.com.
10. National Drug Intelligence Center, *National Drug Threat Assessment 2010*, February 2010. www.justice.gov.
11. Quoted in Christine Lagorio, "Inside a 'Pill Mill,'" CBS News, May 31, 2007. www.cbsnews.com.
12. Quoted in Frank Lombardi, Kerry Burke, and Katie Nelson, "Oxycodone Ring Busted: $1 Million-a-Year Business Run out of Ice Cream Truck on Staten Island," *New York Daily News*, March 17, 2011. www.nydailynews.com.
13. Quoted in Mariana van Zeller, "The Oxycontin Express," *Vanguard*, Current TV, October 15, 2009. http://current.com.

What Are the Health Dangers of Oxycodone Abuse?

14. Purdue Pharma, "OxyContin," 2010. www.purduepharma.com.
15. US National Library of Medicine, "Oxycodone," MedlinePlus, April 25, 2011. www.nlm.nih.gov.
16. Quoted in Kevin Dale, "Pills Take Lethal Local Toll," *Sarasota (FL) Herald-Tribune*, February 10, 2008. www.heraldtribune.com.
17. Quoted in "Hillbilly Heroin," *Intervention*, A&E. www.aetv.com, April 10, 2011.
18. Guest, "Oxycontin Abuse Long Term Problems," SteadyHealth.com, January 28, 2009. www.steadyhealth.com.
19. Quoted in Nick Miroff, "A Dark Addiction," *Washington Post*, January 13, 2008, p. A01.
20. Quoted in Goff, "'I Should Have Been Dead.'"
21. Steve Hayes, "Teen Prescription Drug Abuse," PrescriptionReport.com, March 13, 2008. http://blog.prescriptionreport.com.
22. Quoted in Jennifer Radcliffe, "Students Ill After Pills Given Out 'Like Candy,'" *Houston Chronicle*, January

25, 2009, p. A1.

23. National Drug Intelligence Center, *National Drug Threat Assessment 2010.*

Should the Government Do More to Control Oxycodone?

24. Purdue Pharma, "OxyContin."

25. Prescription Drug Monitoring Program, "Prescription Drug Epidemic in Florida," 2010. http://drugcontrol. flgov.com.

26. Quoted in Jerry Markon, "Despite Probe, Prescription Drug Abuse Worsening, Authorities Say," *Washington Post*, March 14, 2010. www. washingtonpost.com.

27. US Drug Enforcement Administration, "DEA-Led Operation Pill Nation Targets Rogue Pain Clinics in South Florida," news release, February 24, 2011. www.justice.gov.

28. BanOxycontin.com, "Petition to Ban Oxycontin." www.prescriptionaddicti onradio.com/banoxycontin.

How Can Oxycodone Abuse Be Prevented?

29. Quoted in Kevin B. O'Reilly, "Prescription Drug Overdose Cases Sky-rocket at Emergency Departments," *American Medical News*, July 12, 2010. www.ama-assn.org.

30. Quoted in Henry L. Davis, "Controlling Pain Without Creating Addicts," BuffaloNews.com, March 28, 2011. www.buffalonews.com.

31. Quoted in Landers, "Dangerous Diversions."

32. Kevin B. O'Reilly, "Pain Contracts Can Undermine Patient Trust, Critics Say," *American Medical News*, December 27, 2010. www.ama-assn.org.

33. Quoted in Kevin B. O'Reilly, "Opioid Prescribing Requires Close Patient Monitoring," *American Medical News*, March 21, 2011. www.ama-assn.org.

34. National Center on Addiction and Substance Abuse at Columbia University, "The Importance of Family Dinners VI," September 2010. www. casacolumbia.org.

35. Quoted in Dale, "Pills Take Lethal Local Toll."

36. Quoted in Landers, "Dangerous Diversions."

37. Personal conversation with the author, April 6, 2011. Linda's name has been changed at her request.

List of Illustrations

List of Illustrations

Index

Note: Boldface page numbers indicate illustrations.

About the Author

Lydia Bjornlund is a freelance writer and editor living in Northern Virginia. She has written more than two dozen nonfiction books for children and teens, mostly on American history and health-related topics. Bjornlund holds a master's degree in education from Harvard University and a BA in American Studies from Williams College. She lives with her husband, Gerry Hoetmer, and their children, Jake and Sophia.